The World's Monetary System

RETHINKING BRETTON WOODS

Series Editors:
Jo Marie Griesgraber and Bernhard G. Gunter

This series of five books explores a broad range of proposals for achieving more equitable, sustainable and participatory development, particularly through the international financial institutions. The task of the series is to offer the activist and political communities insights into effecting genuine institutional reform over the next 10 to 15 years.

THE WORLD'S MONETARY SYSTEM

Toward Stability and Sustainability in the
Twenty-first Century

Edited by
Jo Marie Griesgraber and Bernhard G. Gunter

Pluto Press
LONDON • CHICAGO, IL.
with
Center of Concern WASHINGTON, DC

First published 1996 by Pluto Press
345 Archway Road, London N6 5AA
and 1436 West Randolph, Chicago, Illinois 60607, USA

British Library Cataloguing in Publication Data
A catalogue record for this book is available from the
British Library

ISBN 0 7453 1052 4 hbk

Library of Congress Cataloging in Publication Data
The world's monetary system : toward stability and sustainability in the
twenty-first century / edited by Jo Marie Griesgraber and Bernhard G.
Gunter.
          p.   cm. — (Rethinking Bretton Woods : v.4)
     Includes bibliographical references and index.
     ISBN 0-7453-1052-4 (hc)
     1. International Monetary Fund. 2. International finance—
History. 3. Economic development—History. I. Griesgraber, Jo
Marie. II. Gunter, Bernhard G., 1964–   .   III. Series.
HG3881.R418 1996   vol. 4
[HG3881.5.I58]
332.1'52—dc20   95–49683
                                                            CIP

Designed, typeset and produced for Pluto Press by
Chase Production Services, Chipping Norton, OX7 5QR
Printed in the EC by J.W. Arrowsmith Ltd, Bristol

Contents

LIST OF TABLES

This volume is dedicated to
GRAHAM BIRD, GERALD HELLEINER, TONY KILLICK
and JOHN WILLIAMSON
in appreciation of their work on the developing countries'
concerns with the international monetary system.

Preface

To explore a broad range of proposals for achieving more equitable, sustainable, and participatory development, particularly through the international financial institutions, the Center of Concern convened a conference in Washington, DC, from June 12–17, 1994. The conference was part of the Rethinking Bretton Woods project, which marked the fiftieth anniversary of the Bretton Woods, New Hampshire, meeting that created the World Bank and the International Monetary Fund (IMF) and laid the groundwork for the General Agreement on Tariffs and Trade (GATT), succeeded by the World Trade Organization (WTO) in 1995.

Conference participants came from 27 countries in Africa, Asia, Australia, Europe, and North and South America, and included economists, historians, sociologists, lawyers, businesspeople, political scientists, theologians, and representatives of the Bretton Woods institutions (BWIs). Their papers and discussions focused on roles for the BWIs – the World Bank, the IMF and the soon-to-be-established WTO – in initiating, assisting and sustaining such development. This series of books originated as the preparatory papers for that conference.

The project's 23 sponsors include persons from academic and non-governmental institutions in 18 countries; an advisory group has members from nine countries. The lead organization, the Center of Concern, is a Washington DC-based social justice research center founded in 1971 to analyze, educate and advocate on issues of international development. Louis Goodman, Dean of the School of International Service at the American University, a project adviser and cosponsor, hosted the conference.

This book is the result of the hard work and generosity of many: the advisers and sponsors of Rethinking Bretton Woods; the funders, the John D. and Catherine T. MacArthur Foundation, the Ford Foundation, the C.S. Mott Foundation, the World

Council of Churches, CEBEMO, Trocaire and CAFOD, and their very competent staffs; the staff and interns of the Center of Concern; the style editors Jane Deren, Renee Y. Storteboom and Marie Walters; and the staff at Pluto Press, Roger van Zwanenberg et al. The editors appreciate deeply the support and good humor of families: Shaw, Andrea, Stanley, David and Jesmin.

Jo Marie Griesgraber
Bernhard G. Gunter
Washington, DC
September 1995

List of Acronyms

ACP	African, Caribbean and Pacific (countries)
ADR	American Depositary Receipt
AfDB	African Development Bank
AsDB	Asian Development Bank
BIS	Bank for International Settlement
BWI	Bretton Woods institution
C–20	Committe of Twenty (Committee on Reform of the International Monetary System and Related Issues)
CAD	EC Capital Adequacy Directive
CCFF	Compensatory and Contingency Financing Facility
EBRD	European Bank for Reconstruction and Development
ECLAC	Economic Commission for Latin America and the Caribbean
ECOSOC	Economic and Social Council
EC	European Community
EDT	external debt stock
EFF	Extended Fund Facility
EMS	European Monetary System
ERP	Economic Reform and Recovery Programme
ESAF	Enhanced Structural Adjustment Facility
FAO	Food and Agriculture Organization
FDI	foreign direct investment
G–5	Group of Five
G–7	Group of Seven
G–10	Group of Ten
G–24	Group of Twenty-four
GAB	General Arrangements to Borrow
GATT	General Agreement on Tariffs and Trade
GDP	gross domestic product
GDR	Global Depositary Receipt

GEF	Global Environment Facility
GNP	gross national product
GRA	General Resources Account
GSP	Generalized System of Preferences
HDI	Human Development Index
HIC	highly indebted country
IBRD	International Bank for Reconstruction and Development
ICSID	International Center for Settlements of Investment Disputes
IDA	International Development Association
IDB	Inter-American Development Bank
IDF	International Debt Facility
IDDF	International Debt Discount Facility
IFC	International Finance Corporation
IFI	international financial institution
ILSA	International Lending Supervisory Act
IMF	International Monetary Fund
ILO	International Labour Organisation
IOSCO	International Organization of Securities Commissions
ITO	International Trade Organization
LDC	less developed country
MDB	Multilateral Development Bank
MIGA	Multilateral Investment Guarantee Agency
NAFTA	North American Free Trade Agreement
NGO	non-governmental organization
ODA	official development assistance
OECD	Organization for Economic Cooperation and Development
OPEC	Organization of Petroleum Exporting Countries
PFP	policy framework paper
PPP	purchasing power parity
SAF	structural adjustment facility
SAL	structural adjustment loan
SAP	structural adjustment program
SDR	special drawing right
SEC	Securities and Exchange Commission
SECAL	sectoral adjustment loan
SID	Society for International Development
SNA	System of National Accounts
SPA	Special Programme of Assistance
TDS	total debt service
TNC	transnational corporation

UNCED	United Nations Conference on Environment and Development
UNCSD	United Nations Commission on Sustainable Development
UNCTAD	United Nations Conference on Trade and Development
UNDP	United Nations Development Programme
UNEP	United Nations Environment Programme
UNESCO	United Nations Educational, Scientific and Cultural Organization
UNICEF	United Nations International Children's Emergency Fund
UNHCR	United Nations High Commission for Refugees
UNSIA	United Nations Security Insurance Agency
WFP	World Food Programme
WHO	World Health Organization
WTO	World Trade Organization

Introduction

A stable and sustainable monetary system is a crucial factor for growth and development. The current international monetary system has been correctly identified as a non-system. It lacks a coherent set of regulations for capital transfers among countries; its variety of exchange-rate arrangements imposes real costs – especially on developing countries – from exchange-rate misalignments and high exchange-rate volatility.

The current variety of exchange-rate arrangements is well documented in the IMF's International Financial Statistics: 24 countries pegged their currencies to the US dollar, 14 countries to the French franc, 8 countries to another single currency, four countries to the Special Drawing Right (SDR) and 25 to baskets of currencies. Another 13 countries have limited their flexibility of exchange rates to either a single currency or within a cooperative arrangement; three countries adjust their exchange rates on the basis of arbitrarily chosen indicators and 24 countries use other managed floating exchange rates. The remaining 55 countries float their exchange rates independently.[1]

This has not always been the case. Beginning with the Paris Conference of 1867, the gold standard provided a relatively fixed exchange rate system until World War I. Efforts to restore the gold standard after World War I failed definitely during the Great Depression. Having learned the high costs of failing to develop rules for economic coordination, delegates from 44 countries reached agreement for a new international monetary system of fixed, but adjustable, exchange rates, the so-called Bretton Woods system in 1944. The Bretton Woods system ended August 15, 1971, when US President Nixon terminated the guarantee to exchange one ounce of gold for US$35. The economic record of the Bretton Woods system (1945–71) is impressive: 'Advanced industrial countries grew nearly twice as rapidly as in any comparable period before or since.'[2]

Growth rates of most developing countries continued to be high over the next few years, but turned negative after August 12, 1982, when Mexico declared a moratorium on its debt service payments, officially heralding the start of the debt crisis. Although it would not be appropriate to see the collapse of the Bretton Woods system as the main cause of the debt crisis, there is little doubt that the debt crisis was influenced by an unstable international monetary system.

Nevertheless, even without a coherent exchange-rate arrangement since the end of the Bretton Woods era, the financial system has become more global and the world economy more integrated. However, the globalization of the international financial system and the integration of the world economy have not been without costs. The international monetary system has become a fragile, unstable and, in the long run, unsustainable system. As Moises Naim illustrated, although mismanagement and speculation played an important role in the Mexico peso crisis, Mexico was also a victim of the current international financial non-system.[3]

The International Monetary Fund (IMF), whose initial core function had been to maintain the Bretton Woods par value system, has adjusted to other roles in the international economy. However, none is as crucial as that original role. This volume applies to the IMF the principles and paradigms set forth in Volumes I and II of this series on Rethinking Bretton Woods; those same principles and paradigms were applied to the World Bank in Volume III, and will be applied to world trade in Volume V.

Volume IV commences the necessary discussion on how to move the international monetary system toward stability and sustainability in the twenty-first century. The consensus that the present non-system needs change goes unchallenged. Authors from Belgium, Chile, Germany, India and the United States concur. However, befitting discussions early in the process, their various proposals are not necessarily consistent with each other.

Chapter 1, by Robert S. Browne, explores the contemporary needs of the international monetary system and compares them to the present mandate and operations of the International Monetary Fund. After a short historical review of the IMF, he analyzes the current main problems of the IMF. He then offers a visionary alternative to the existing IMF, followed by a pragmatic alternative. He recognizes the asymmetry between borrowers and non-borrowers and makes a series of politically feasible proposals to prepare the IMF for the twenty-first century. Browne's extensive experience, both as a US Executive Director to the African Development Bank and as a Staff Director on the US House of Representatives' Banking Committee's Subcommittee on International Development, is evident as he describes the political pitfalls to reform.

In Chapter 2, Sunanda Sen reviews the developing countries' limited access to IMF drawing rights, and then analyzes various debt-reduction schemes, particularly the Brady Plan. She examines the adequacy of concerted lendings by private banks or official agencies, via debt forgiveness or the menu-based voluntary approaches. She concludes the chapter with a proposal that global Keynesianism shape a new mandate for the IMF, a proposal expected to contribute greatly toward sustainable development. Sen's analysis derives from many years of teaching and research at leading universities in India and the United Kingdom, including the Jawaharlal Nehru University in New Delhi, and Oxford University.

Chapter 3, by Stephany Griffith-Jones with Vassilis Papageorgiou, opens with a description of recent trends in private financial markets. It goes on to analyze the structural changes in global private financial markets – particularly resulting from deregulation and liberalization – and evaluates their benefits and costs. Based on this analysis, she defines the increase and change in the nature of risk, with special reference to risks as they affect less developed countries (LDCs). The chapter then reviews some of the main aspects of the supervisory and regulatory responses to the changes in financial flows and, above all, to changes in perceived risk which they generate. It concludes by proposing policy recommendations, arranged from those which are more widely accepted (but not implemented) to those which are more innovative. One of the strongest suggestions is in support of the Tobin tax on speculative capital flows, a proposal which recurs like a musical theme throughout many of the chapters in this volume. The proposals offered here could be said to reflect an emerging consensus among international agencies on options for the international financial system, since Griffith-Jones has worked for most of those agencies: a Senior Fellow at the Institute of Development Studies, Sussex University, UK, she has worked at the Central Bank of Chile and as a senior consultant to the UN Economic Commission for Latin America and the Caribbean (ECLAC), the World Bank, the Inter-American Development Bank, the European Economic Community, and the UN Conference on Trade and Development (UNCTAD).

Avadhoot R. Nadkarni analyzes in Chapter 4 the preferences of the LDCs for fixity in exchange-rate arrangements. Based on these preferences, Nadkarni calls for the establishment of fixed nominal parities as a precondition for the policy coordination that would need to precede the ultimate establishment of a more efficient governance of the world economy. He then brings out some of the real costs of excessive devaluations of LDC currencies and discusses the compensations that should be paid to the LDCs for these devaluations. The international asset to pay for such compensations is discussed before he summarizes his main proposals. Nadkarni, who teaches economics at St Xavier's College, Bombay, and the University of Bombay, derives his sophisticated analysis from India's experience with devaluation and liberalization.

Bernard Lietaer reviews the characteristics, advantages and disadvantages of three possible types of global reference currency in Chapter 5. He introduces a commodity-backed global currency with the additional feature of a time-related holding charge (demurrage charge) and analyzes its implications for the business cycle, employment, inflation, the environment and international business. He describes historical precedents for such a charge currency and confronts potential misunderstandings of the concept. The cross-temporal, multi-disciplinary flavour of this chapter reflects the author's varied background. A native of Belgium, he has lived in Grand Cayman Island where he was president of Pegasys Currency Fund, and earlier of Pegasys Management Ltd; he previously was general manager and currency trader for Gaia-Corp, and headed the organization and planning department of the Belgian Central Bank. He holds degrees in electrical engineering and business administration, and taught international finance at the University of Louvain.

Chapter 6 provides a useful review and critique of the various reform proposals for the international monetary system, both those included in this volume and those discussed in the professional literature. Gunter, a German national, is one of the editors for the Rethinking Bretton Wood series and a Ph.D. candidate in Economics at the American University in Washington, DC. He argues that a single world currency, issued by a World Central Bank, is the first best solution. He carefully unmasks the principal fallacious arguments against a World Central Bank.

Since these essays were commissioned, several significant events have occurred relating to the future of the IMF, and perhaps of the international monetary system. As Naim noted, the Mexican peso collapse revealed 'the fault lines underlying current trends in global economics and politics'.[4] The US government enlisted the IMF to join in the rescue of the peso – an action that provoked resentment among other Fund shareholders, who accused the United States of using the Fund for its bilateral foreign policy objectives. Mexican after-shocks were felt within the Fund, where an internal study challenged the Fund's own 'cult of secrecy', and outside the Fund, particularly at the G–7 Economic Summit in Halifax, June 1995. There the Fund was admonished to undertake more substantive surveillance, including capital accounts as well as current accounts in its review; to speak candidly with governments pursuing inappropriate policies; and to collect more and more timely data from governments. The G–7 hoped to avoid future Mexico-style crises by increasing the quality of surveillance, and then to meet any future crisis with adequate resources through: (a) an increase in quotas; (b) a Special Drawing Right (SDR) allocation that could be distributed according to new and as yet to be determined criteria; and (c) a new Emergency Financing Facility for countries with sound economic policies which are experiencing a speculative assault on their currency. The G–7 also proposed that the G–10 coordinate their regulations regarding securities, bonds, and mutual funds, that is, the debts to individuals that Mexico was unable to service.

For the first time the G–7 also suggested that the World Bank and the IMF recognize that countries were having problems servicing their multilateral debt, and to take steps to resolve those debt problems. Shortly before the Autumn 1995 World Bank/ IMF Annual Meetings, the press reported on a leaked Bank study calling for a new Multilateral Debt Facility. According to the plan, once debtor countries had loan reduction arrangements in place with their commercial and bilateral official creditors, this new facility would pay the debt service (principal plus interest) on the debtor's multilateral debt as it came due. The multilateral debt included that owed to the IMF, the World Bank and the regional development banks.

These events demonstrate that reform of the IMF and the international monetary system is a dynamic and timely topic. This volume has presented sound analysis with creative and well-founded proposals for reform. Whether future reality will conform to these proposals is not knowable. However, these proposals set a standard for evaluating changes consistent with promoting a more equitable, participatory and sustainable global economic system.

Notes

1. International Monetary Fund (IMF), *International Financial Statistics*, vol. 47/7 (Washington, DC: IMF, July 1994), p. 8.
2. Barry Eichengreen and Peter B. Kenen, 'Managing the World Economy under the Bretton Woods System: An Overview' in Peter B. Kenen (ed.), *Managing the World Economy: Fifty Years after Bretton Woods* (Washington, DC: Institute for International Economics, 1994), p. 3.
3. Moises Naim, 'Mexico's Larger Story' in *Foreign Policy*, vol. 112 (Summer 1995), pp. 112–30.
4. Naim, 'Mexico's Larger Story', p. 112.

1 Rethinking the IMF on Its Fiftieth Anniversary

Robert S. Browne

INTRODUCTION

The International Monetary Fund (IMF) and the World Bank were created simultaneously at an international conference held in 1944 in Bretton Woods, New Hampshire. Convened while World War II was still raging, but after the Allies had finally begun to feel some assurance that victory would be theirs, the Conference reflected the widely held concern that the victors reach some agreement on the structure of the post-war global economy. The international economic behavior which had characterized the inter-war period left much to be desired. Indeed, many scholars attributed the roots of World War II to the faulty economic relationships instituted after World War I. Wisdom dictated that the most propitious moment for reaching a new accommodation was before the cooperative atmosphere of the allied war effort gave way to the narrow nationalistic concerns likely to re-emerge once peace was established.

The stated objectives of the IMF were to promote and maintain high levels of employment and income through the expansion of international trade and the achievement and maintenance of exchange-rate stability and currency convertibility. The basic structure given to the IMF was suggestive of a credit union to which member countries make their contributions (in gold and national currency) of a size determined by the magnitude of their national wealth and economic activity, and from which they might borrow, should their national finances deteriorate to the point where a threat existed to their ability to maintain the agreed exchange rate of their currency. The newly designed international monetary system designated the US dollar, backed by gold, as the anchor currency against which all exchange rates were calibrated. A major task for the IMF was to extend loans to enable borrowers to work out short-term imbalances in their current accounts. These loans were generally of short maturity and were conditioned on the borrower making necessary adjustments to enable its economy to return to a stable position. Should a member country find that it was facing a payments imbalance of such severity that, even with a loan, it could not continue to function with the prevailing exchange rate, the IMF could agree to a permanent change in that country's exchange rate. In its early years, the principal borrowers were industrialized countries.

In terms of its stated objectives, the IMF's performance can be rated as generally favorable over its first 25 years. Exchange rates were kept reasonably stable and international trade enjoyed an era of unprecedented growth. The poorer countries complained, with some justification, that the international monetary system was biased against them. Even the developed countries, as their economies returned to normalcy, balked over the advantages which flowed to the United States as a result of the system's use of the dollar as the anchor, or reserve currency. These grumblings became louder as the United States ran up an astronomical budget deficit in order to finance the Vietnam War, a war which had little support among the other industrialized nations. These nations complained that they were, in effect, involuntarily helping to finance the conflict because of their obligation to maintain their currencies in a fixed relationship with a dollar which was rapidly depreciating in terms of the gold into which it was allegedly convertible.

By 1971, the fictitious relationship between gold and the dollar had become so untenable that President Nixon abruptly closed the gold window. That is, he ended the dollar's convertibility into gold, and later decreased its official gold content. This formally terminated the era of fixed exchange rates and introduced floating rate options for all IMF member states.

The net effect of these radical alterations in the exchange-rate system left the IMF with a very indistinct mandate. Deprived of its principal compass, stable exchange rates, it was not clear just how the vessel was to be steered, or indeed, whether there was any further need for the vessel at all. The major powers, using various forms of informal groupings like the Group of Ten (G–10), Group of Five (G–5), and lately, the Group of Seven (G–7), gradually worked out an informal cooperative arrangement for the management of their monetary relationships. At annual Economic Summit meetings and *ad hoc* interim consultations, the major industrialized nations effectively determined what global monetary arrangements were to be. The role of the IMF had been eclipsed, if not usurped.

AN INTERNATIONAL MONETARY SYSTEM FOR THE TWENTY-FIRST CENTURY

Current Problems

Although the IMF lost much of its *raison d'etre* as a result of the demise of the fixed exchange-rate system, the institution's relevance is currently questioned for reasons that go far beyond the technical activity of exchange-rate management. The explosive expansion of the global economy, the quadrupling numbers of independent countries, the plethora of rising global economic actors such as the transnational corporation and the Eurodollar market, the breathtaking advances in communications technology, and the pressure of an enormous and intransigent developing country debt, are only a few new factors whose impact on the global economy create pressure for reconceptualization of the global monetary institution most appropriate for today's world.

There is also a crescendo of criticism of *how* the IMF pursues its operations under its existing mandate. During the many years when the Fund's lending was directed principally toward the developed countries, complaints about the Fund's structure and operations were muted. Perhaps the disproportionate power wielded by the United States was resented, but inasmuch as the IMF was basically a club of the rich nations, disagreements among peers were handled discreetly and rarely became the focus of popular national discontent. As the Fund's clientele shifted from the developed countries to the developing ones, however, complaints about the IMF's operations escalated *pari passu*.

These complaints against the IMF can be grouped into two categories: those arising from the intrinsic inadequacy of the IMF's mandate, and those focusing on the structural and operational deficiencies in the way the IMF carries out that mandate. Both shortcomings prevent the IMF from fulfilling its limited role as monetary steward for the international community.

The conceptual inadequacies are the absence of:

- an independent (country-neutral) reserve currency,

- a mechanism to stabilize exchange rates,

- a mechanism to provide macroeconomic direction to the global economy and

- a lender of last resort.

The structural and operational deficiencies are:

- an undemocratic voting structure,

- an absence of public participation and excessive confidentiality,

- an asymmetry in the IMF's control over members' policies,

- medium-term loans used for long-term needs,

- the duplication of development work of the World Bank,

- the freeze on issuance of Special Drawing Rights (SDRs) and

- the irrational allocation of SDRs.

The conceptual inadequacies can be resolved only by replacing the IMF by a new supra-national entity empowered to influence global economic policy without constraints imposed by conflicting national interests – much as a strong central bank operates independently of its nation's executive branch. The achievement of a global consensus necessary to create such an entity probably lies in the distant future, although the urgency for moving forward with some sort of supra-national economic entity may be felt sooner than one would expect.

The structural and operational deficiencies lend themselves to modification within the framework of the IMF as it is now conceived. Although some of these modifications, especially the introduction of a more democratic voting policy, would certainly entail some reshaping of the institution, they would leave intact the IMF's present conceptualization as an institution seeking to coordinate and harmonize the interests of its sovereign member states.

Regardless of how the voting structure were modified, however, the IMF's policies would continue to reflect the policies demanded by the dominant voting bloc within the governing body.

A Visionary Alternative to the Existing IMF

Before proceeding to an examination of the flaws in the IMF's present structure and operations, let us first examine some of its conceptual inadequacies and reflect on what a vision of an appropriate global monetary entity might entail. The last 25 years of experience, as the IMF has wrestled with the host of new, and newly identified, factors exerting an impact on international affairs, have demonstrated the inadequacy of the IMF as a monetary institution for bringing economic stability and growth to today's global community. This inadequacy was glimpsed at Bretton Woods, where the birth of the IMF was marked by controversy: questions arose about whether the tasks being assigned to it were sufficiently comprehensive to meet the world's monetary needs. The English economist John Maynard Keynes argued that the global community needed a more far-reaching monetary institution than the IMF, an institution which would have the ability to issue its own currency and to function much as a global central bank. Keynes seems to have foreseen that the attempt to use the currency of a particular country as the reserve currency for the world would prove to be non-viable over the long term.[1]

Not surprisingly, as the United States lost its position of unrivaled economic strength *vis-a-vis* other major countries, it also progressively lost its claim to unchallenged global monetary leadership. This weakness became more apparent as the United States' acquiescence in ongoing balance-of-payments deficits gradually transformed the United States from a creditor to a debtor nation. Furthermore, the use of the dollar as the international reserve currency imposed awkward strictures on the United States' ability to manage its domestic economy. This handicap was balanced by the tremendous advantage which the United States derived from its unique entitlement to issue unlimited amounts of its currency and oblige other countries to hold it.

A number of events suggest that change is long overdue. Now is the time to replace the remnants of this clumsy, largely defunct, system by the creation of a global central bank, authorized to issue currency in its own name. Although this would be a radical change from present monetary arrangements, it would offer a high potential for addressing some of the ills which plague the current international monetary system. Replacing the dollar with a neutral reserve currency could, by itself, introduce a greater measure of equity to the relations between the poorer and the richer countries. Utilizing the dollar as the reserve currency unavoidably links the fate of virtually all countries, especially the poorer ones, to the economic policies pursued by the United States. For example, when the United States delinked the dollar from gold and devalued it, the countries holding their reserves in dollars sustained serious losses, whereas those which could afford to hold their reserves in gold experienced tremendous windfalls. Although this was a unique event, other examples can be cited of negative consequences for other countries arising from the system's use of a country-based reserve currency. The reserve currency tends to become the principal monetary medium for conducting international trade, thereby enhancing the economic strength of the issuing country *vis-a-vis* other countries, but especially *vis-a-vis* the poorer ones. Poor countries are also less able than rich ones to hedge their own monetary transactions against fluctuations in the value of the reserve currency.

The vulnerability of the existing system was never in greater evidence than in September of 1992, when a private American financial institution, engaging in currency speculation for private gain, managed to inflict several billion dollars in losses on the powerful Bank of England, precipitating a stiff devaluation of the British pound and forcing that once-proud currency out of the incipient European currency union. The American speculator is reported to have made one billion dollars in profit, and the European exchange markets were thrown into total disarray by the incident. If the existing monetary arrangements cannot protect strong national currencies from such private speculation, it is unlikely that any type of entity of less than supra-national status can do so. A global central bank could certainly devise tools to counter such destabilizing activities. Similarly, the phenomenon of the transnational corporation, a rootless profit-seeking entity which knows no nationality but is capable of moving vast amounts of investment capital around the globe in an endless search for maximum profits, constitutes another supra-national threat to the maintenance of global economic stability. This threat can only be countered by another supra-national entity such as a global central bank.

The mere thought of so powerful an institution as a global central bank is, of course, cause for considerable concern. It must be pointed out, however, that a mild, if unpredictable, form of global macroeconomic policy is already being practiced by the G–7 nations, who periodically attempt to implement coordinated monetary policies with a view to achieving macroeconomic outcomes which they have mutually agreed on. In the Bretton Woods conceptualization, this was to be the task of the IMF. If the IMF finds that it can no longer carry out this task, then a more appropriate institution is called for. Abdicating this responsibility to the G–7 not only introduces an element of unaccountability to the process, it undermines the very concept of a global democratic order.

However, a global central bank could function only if its member countries were prepared to yield to it some degree of sovereignty in the exercise of economic policy. For instance, countries enjoying payments surpluses or experiencing unusually high growth rates would, on occasion, be obliged to restrain their economies in order to bring about greater stability in the global economy. This could entail such politically sensitive trade-offs as dampening the economic activity of one country to stimulate the economy of another country. But the question is: do countries exist which are today prepared to accede to such a surrender of sovereignty?

A global central bank, as provider of international reserves and as lender of last resort, would be in a position to play a powerful role in shaping the economic profile of the global economic community. In deciding how it would distribute reserves, it could choose among a host of formulae, depending on the desired objectives, just as the IMF, when creating SDRs, decided to channel the bulk of them toward the richer countries, although they needed them least.

Theoretically, the new global central bank could distribute liquidity in ways which would help to achieve whatever policy results it wished. In practice, of course, the central bank would be only a tool of its members, and the policies followed would reflect the wishes of those members. There is, therefore, no guarantee that the global central bank would not mimic the IMF and become the tool of the rich nations. Whether it is possible to impose a distribution of power within a global financial institution that contradicts the distribution of wealth and power in the external world is, of course, the issue underlying this entire discussion.

The imperatives of the current human condition may call for

the creation of a global central bank, but the likelihood that any significant number of the industrialized nations would, in the foreseeable future, yield the sovereignty necessary for its operation is very slim indeed. The ever-increasing evidence that the present system is badly in need of repair or replacement is so overwhelming, however, that it is almost certain that within the next few years some change in the collective management of global affairs, including monetary affairs, will be seen. Given this scenario, some visionary thinking is probably not inappropriate.

A Pragmatic Alternative to the Existing IMF

If the global central bank is at present little more than a visionary hope, then we are left with the more immediate task of refashioning the IMF with a view to making it a more effective vehicle for providing international monetary stewardship in the near term.

Perhaps there is no better means of approaching this topic than by examining the distribution of power within the IMF. Voting is based upon each country's quota. An IMF quota is primarily an indicator of how much money a country antes up to the IMF's treasury: thus the richer the country, the larger its quota is likely to be. There is a certain logic to this linkage between contributions and votes because the IMF is a lending institution, and lenders are expected to demand some degree of control over the use of their funds. On the other hand, much lip service is paid these days to the concept of democracy. If it is to have any meaning whatsoever, democracy cannot be reconciled with a situation where the vast majority of countries are denied any real influence over so vital an economic instrument as international monetary policy. The IMF's undemocratic nature is even more sharply exposed by the fact that, for the approval of certain important issues, a majority vote of as much as 85 per cent is required for passage.[2] While it may be unrealistic to expect the industrialized countries to place their funds into a one-country one-vote structure, it is not unreasonable to expect a more democratic arrangement than that which exists at present. Nor is it unreasonable to demand that the inner deliberations of the IMF be more open to public scrutiny and participation than is now the case. A valid argument can be made for a certain amount of confidentiality surrounding high-level negotiations at the international level, and for preventing speculators from having premature knowledge of pending changes in policy. These considerations can be respected without resorting to the high degree of secrecy which characterizes the IMF's operations.

Another egregious example of the inequitable treatment of poor and rich countries in the IMF relates to the degree of compliance exacted for IMF directives, or what IMF critics refer to as the 'asymmetry problem'. Although considerable publicity is given to the often controversial conditionalities which the IMF imposes upon its borrowers, it is less well known that the economies of the non-borrowing countries are also subjected to regular surveillance by IMF staff. Following each such surveillance, the IMF makes strong representations to all countries whose economic policies are perceived as being harmful to the global economy. Countries with persistent balance-of-payments surpluses or deficits are urged to reduce them; countries with persistent budget deficits are urged to eliminate them.

The asymmetry comes from the fact that, where borrowing countries are concerned, the IMF insists that the policies which it recommends be carried out or the erring borrower will face the loss of its loan. With the non-borrowers, however, the IMF can do little more than urge that the recommended policies be followed. It lacks any mechanism for insuring that its policy recommendations will be implemented by non-borrowers, and it is common for non-borrowers to ignore them entirely. The United States is a prime example of this phenomenon. For years the IMF has highlighted various nefarious global effects arising from the persistent US budget deficit. It has publicly urged Washington to reduce it, all to no effect. If a poor, famine-stricken country in Africa is expected to slash its budget deficit when its people are already at the brink of disaster, why shouldn't the United States be expected to do the same, especially if its deficit is hurting other, less fortunate countries?

Actually, this asymmetry is doubly objectionable, because bad policies pursued by the industrialized countries frequently have strongly negative effects on the poorer countries, whereas the bad policies pursued by the poor countries generally damage only themselves. Asymmetry undermines the credibility of the Fund and is a manifestation of the sovereignty problem cited earlier as the principal obstacle to the establishment of a global central bank. It could, of course, be resolved – if the will to do so existed.

As mentioned, the emergence of the debt crisis in 1982 afforded the IMF an opportunity to again become a major player on the international economic scene, after losing its mandate in 1971 to maintain fixed exchange rates. The fact that it disposed of only short-term funds did not daunt IMF staff. Not surprisingly, the IMF rapidly became the focus of considerable protest because the short-term nature of its funds led it to demand that policy reforms be implemented within unrealistic time frames, thereby producing serious negative effects within the borrowing countries. Eventually, however, the IMF managed to win authorization from its members to provide medium-term loans. Faced with the prospect of serious defaults from insolvent countries, it created the Structural Adjustment Facility (SAF) and later the Enhanced Structural Adjustment Facility (ESAF), both of which served as vehicles for rolling over the IMF's shorter-term, near-market rate loans into medium-term maturities at very modest rates of interest.

By this time, however, the World Bank, which is a development agency and well supplied with long-term loan funds, had also entered the debt amelioration business. The World Bank extended what were known as structural adjustment loans (SALs) to the debt-strapped countries. Unlike the Bank's normal project loans, which were designated for such identifiable items as roads and bridges, SALs could be used for reducing balance-of-payments deficits, for debt-servicing and for the purchase of imports. However, qualification for SALs required the adoption of strong policy reforms reminiscent of the conditionalities imposed earlier by the IMF's stabilization loans.

Indeed, it was not long before the work of the two institutions converged to the point where much of their work was virtually indistinguishable. Questions arose as to why two bureaucracies were needed to plough the same ground. Meanwhile, environmental groups and other interested non-governmental organizations (NGOs) – who for many years had been pushing demands that the World Bank take human rights, environmental impacts, poverty and other social criteria into consideration in approving its project loans – soon realized that such demands also needed to be directed toward the IMF. The IMF, however, is ill-staffed to meet these demands owing to the narrowly specialized nature of its professional staff, virtually all of whom are economists. To gear up to respond to these demands would entail the hiring of specialists from a host of additional disciplines, thus creating a second expensive bureaucracy parallel to that of the World Bank.

Inasmuch as the Bank is the agency designated to do development lending, there is little justification for the Fund to duplicate that task. This is not to suggest that the two institutions should merge, although there is a growing chorus calling for such an action.[3] Monetary issues are distinct from development issues, and the Fund has proved itself well equipped to deal with the former, but ill-equipped to deal with the latter. The Fund needs to find a means to reinsert itself into monetary policy. The need for an international monetary institution has certainly not disappeared. Despite the prevalence of floating exchange rates, countries continue to find themselves in temporary need of funds to carry them through short-term payments imbalances. An IMF-like institution is vitally needed to assist in such circumstances.

Perhaps even more vital, however, is the role which the Fund could play in facilitating the widespread use of a country-neutral reserve currency. The SDR, although falling short of being the international currency which Keynes envisioned before and during the Bretton Woods conference, has performed an important service by familiarizing the world with the concept of an independent reserve currency. Unfortunately, the failure to continue to expand its usage and to introduce it more visibly into the public consciousness, has rendered it virtually ineffectual. The need for such a currency instrument has not disappeared, however, and the IMF is derelict in not pushing its usage more vigorously. The IMF is, of course, the instrument of its wealthy members, and it can be paralyzed by the opposition of these members, and especially by the veto power of the United States. The solution to this latter problem lies with mobilizing US Congressional support to push the US Treasury Department toward new monetary initiatives. In so far as developing a greater receptivity to the SDR is concerned, however, most members of the US Congress have probably never heard of an SDR, so that struggle could be long and arduous.

In any case, the struggle should not be simply for more SDRs, but for a more relevant SDR. When SDRs were first created it was mandated that they be distributed to countries on the basis of their quotas within the IMF. If one believes that it is in the best interest of the 'haves' to lend a helping hand to the 'have-nots', then a splendid opportunity was thereby missed for helping to close the intractable gap between the richer and the poorer countries. It was the influential IMF members' own arbitrary action which decided that quotas should be the basis for SDR distributions. A needs-determined basis could just as well have been chosen and, indeed, was requested by the developing countries. The response of the rich countries was that the SDR was

11

intended solely as a mechanism for providing liquidity and should not be linked to welfare considerations of any sort. Later, when the big powers decided to block further issuance of SDRs despite the pleas of the poor countries that they were experiencing severe liquidity shortages, the rationale offered was that the SDR was intended solely as a means for preventing global liquidity shortages. Since there was no longer a *global* shortage, no further SDRs were needed. The fact that many of the member countries were suffering from enormous national liquidity shortages was treated as irrelevant.

In 1987, a bill was offered in the US House of Representatives instructing the US Treasury Department to raise with the IMF the idea of making a one-time issuance of 'limited purpose' SDRs,[4] which would be allocated among the poorest of the debt-burdened countries on a needs-determined basis, with the limited purpose of repaying official debt. The proposition presented an innovative and relatively burdenless means of effectively writing down a significant portion of the developing countries' debt. Unfortunately, the bill was emasculated in subcommittee, and as finally passed,[5] merely mandated the US Treasury Department to prepare a study of the proposal. This effectively killed it, because the US Treasury Department was adamantly opposed to the further issuance of any SDRs whatsoever, even of the orthodox type. None the less, this proposal continues to offer a concrete method for engaging in some serious debt reduction and deserves to be revived. Nor is it entirely clear why the United States, after supporting the creation of the SDR initially, has been so opposed to any expansion of its usage. Alarm in Washington at the prospect of a gradual usurpation of the role of the dollar by the SDR may provide a partial explanation, although the decline in the dollar's hegemony is so inevitable that US interests would probably be best served in the long run if the dollar were to be replaced by an international currency unit rather than by one or more national currencies.

CONCLUSION

It has become fashionable to demonize the IMF, a practice which is not particularly helpful in understanding what the IMF is, what it is meant to achieve, and what its future direction should be. It is most frequently criticized for the harsh policies it imposes on poor countries seeking to borrow from it. Considerable criticism is indeed warranted in this regard, because the IMF has taken an excessively economistic approach to the problems of the poor countries, often demonstrating a total insensitivity to the social and political realities within these countries. The time frame within which it has expected policy reforms to be implemented has generally been unrealistic. Too frequently the IMF has found itself to be a net recipient of capital from the Third World rather than a net exporter of capital to it. Happily, the IMF has taken some limited steps to respond to these criticisms, by softening its lending terms and extending its payback period. Many of these criticisms arise from the fact that the IMF's reserves and its structure were not designed for the type of medium-term (essentially development) lending in which it now finds itself immersed. It would be well advised to leave these activities to the World Bank.

Relinquishing its development lending activities to the World Bank would not leave the Fund with nothing to do. Rather, it would free it to refocus its attention on global monetary affairs. The demise of fixed exchange rates did indeed eliminate the main role which the IMF had been playing in the international monetary system. It did not, however, leave it powerless to play *some* role, if its major members would permit it to do so. Whether by design or by chance, the existing global economic system favors the rich countries over the poor ones. After three so-called 'development decades', the gap between per capita incomes in the poor countries and the rich ones is even larger than at the outset. This is an immoral as well as a dangerous situation, which the world has been too slow in addressing effectively. The monetary system by itself cannot solve this problem but it can be structured to assist in the solution. It should definitely not be an obstacle to its resolution. The IMF recently demonstrated its willingness to break with orthodoxy when it introduced a new method of calculating country GDP figures, utilizing as a basis the purchasing power of a country's currency rather than its official exchange rate with the dollar. This is a significant move toward reality. Only an entity with the stature of the IMF could have institutionalized so novel an idea, despite the fact that the concept has been under discussion in academic circles for many years. A logical next step might be for the IMF to test the feasibility of an entirely new type of international currency, one which would maintain a constant purchasing power, based perhaps on a basket of commodities.[6]

More democratic voting arrangements and less secrecy about

its inner workings would enhance the IMF's credibility in most of the world, and would be in keeping with the current shift toward more democracy at the national level in many countries. However, the asymmetry problem, which is just another form of discriminatory treatment favoring the richer countries, is not likely to be resolved soon. The rich countries will probably continue to ignore the IMF's strictures until a new, more effective supranational structure is imposed or agreed to.

These suggested adjustments in the way the IMF operates, although offering prospects for genuine improvement in the IMF's effectiveness and usefulness to the global community, will not be sufficient to meet the fast-changing needs of the global society of the twenty-first century. For this, an entirely new mindset must be nurtured, one which accepts the inescapable interconnectedness of the human condition everywhere in the world. This realization will ultimately drive society toward the fashioning of global, rather than exclusively national, approaches to problem solving. The need will then become apparent for the nation state to sacrifice some of its sovereignty in the interest of achieving a greater good. The achievement of consensus on the fashioning of a supra-national monetary institution would be a necessary component of building such a global community. One aspect of preparing the public for such a step would be for the IMF to move the SDR out of the closet and accustom people to the concept of a global currency. Americans and others were gradually brought to accept a paper dollar whose value rests solely on its public acceptance rather than on any intrinsic physical backing. The same can be done for the concept of an internationally issued currency, but it will require considerable time. The sooner we begin, the better.

Space does not allow for a detailed discussion of the myriad facets of a supra-national financial institution, or global central bank. It may, however, be helpful to anticipate some of the concerns likely to be expressed by those seeking to evaluate the merits of such an institution: sovereignty, allocation of power, and funding. There is little which can be predicted with regard to the yielding of national sovereignty to an international body. It is likely to be agreed to by a significant number of nations only when the global monetary system finds itself in a prolonged crisis from which there appears to be no alternate escape.

The other two concerns can be addressed simultaneously. Because most international institutions are financed by their member states, they are usually structured so that the allocation of power within the institution roughly parallels the financial contributions of its member states.[7] This is not a very democratic outcome, of course, and the best way around it is to find another means for funding the institution. One possible source for funding a supranational monetary institution would be from the imposition of a small tax on international monetary transfers of all types.[8] Because such transfers now run into the trillions of dollars annually, a very tiny tax would yield a very large revenue. Such a tax would not be a serious burden for international trade, inasmuch as in excess of 90 per cent of contemporary international financial monetary transfers arise not from trade but from speculative movements of capital, some of which may be useful but many of which may actually be harmful to the international monetary system. Other possible sources of financing could be from the revenues yielded from the exploitation of some of the 'international commons', such as the oceans and the poles.[9] Such non-nation-based funding would go far to counter the pressure for control of the global central bank by the richer countries.

The ways in which we have approached international monetary arrangements in the past must give way to creative new thinking about how humankind can best organize itself for survival in the twenty-first century. The nations of the world must prepare themselves for bold new initiatives, just as they did in Bretton Woods, in 1944.

Notes

1. John M. Keynes, *The Collected Writings of John Maynard Keynes* (Cambridge, England: Macmillan and Cambridge University Press, 1980) vols. 25 and 26.
2. The United States has 17 per cent of the votes in the IMF's governing board, and is thus able to exercise a veto over major policy issues coming before the IMF.
3. See Box 14 of the Staff Review in Bretton Woods Commission, *Bretton Woods: Looking to the Future* (Washington, DC: Bretton Woods Commission, 1994) p. B–20 for further arguments and references why the IMF and the World Bank should not be merged.
4. The 'limited purpose' SDRs would be interest-free for the first user, which is a heavily indebted country. After its first usage, the 'limited purpose' SDR would become a regular SDR.
5. US Congress, *Trade and International Economic Policy Reform Act of 1987*, Title IV, Subtitle A, Chapter 2, section 421.
6. See, for example, Arjun Makhijani and Robert S. Browne 'The World's Monetary Arrangements: Restructuring the International

Monetary System' in *World Policy Journal*, vol. 3/1 (Winter 1985–86) pp. 59–80.

7. The UN General Assembly is a major exception to this pattern.

8. See, for example, James Tobin, 'A Proposal for International Monetary Reform' in *Eastern Economic Journal*, vol. 4, no. 3–4 (July/October 1978) pp. 153–9 and Tobin's more recent proposal in United Nations Development Programme (UNDP) *Human Development Report 1994* (New York: Oxford University Press, 1994) p. 70.

9. For further examples see Norman Girvan, 'Empowerment for Development: From Conditionality to Partnership' in Jo Marie Griesgraber and Bernhard G. Gunter (eds), *Promoting Development: Effective Global Institutions for the Twenty-first Century*, Chapter 2 (London: Pluto Press, 1995) pp. 23–37; or UNDP, *Human Development Report*, p. 69.

2 Debt, Development and the International Monetary Fund

Sunanda Sen

INTRODUCTION

Waves of international capital flows, which made their appearance during the middle of the last century, were matched by commensurate growth of output. This pattern reflected a symbiotic relation between finance and the real economy. Although the pattern disappeared in the first half of the twentieth century, it reappeared after World War II in Europe and Japan: Europe was helped by the Marshall Plan to reconstruct itself and Japan was able to access an ample supply of external finance.

During these years, imports of capital were fraught with less uncertainty regarding their final destination and their impact on the real sectors of the host economy compared to the pattern prevailing today. Of late, flows of international capital have ceased to operate in the real sector. Thus, these flows follow paths which tend to have little or no impact on material transactions. Furthermore, a boom in finance, aided by an inflow of capital from abroad, often continues in a stagnating real economy.

The close link between capital imports and domestic economic growth was again disrupted during the 1970s, when the oil-importing developing countries refinanced their enhanced import bill by international borrowing. These capital flows were readily intermediated by private banks, which recycled the swelling deposits of the newly rich OPEC countries.

As the debt held by the non-oil-developing-country borrowers accumulated, only a few countries were able to develop the resources for future debt servicing. The steep hikes in real interest rates and the adverse movements in their terms of trade during the 1980s created problems which were further aggravated by the rising value of the US dollar. For some debtors it was a debt trap: these countries had to find additional funds from abroad, through borrowings, refinancings and reschedulings, just to honor their debt-service commitments. The difficulties worsened as the debtor countries experienced problems in securing external finance beyond that needed for their debt servicings. With the emergence of the debt crisis (1982), private capital flows to the developing countries ceased. Since then the world has witnessed a steady growth in security and bond finance, largely confined to the industrial areas. Bank credit, which grew less, also remained within the rich industrial economies.

Developing countries' borrowings have been used mostly to fund debt servicings. Inadequate external finance has led these economies to an alternative route to debt servicings, namely extractions of real transfers, especially through forced cuts in domestic expenditure. Efforts to maintain international creditworthiness by avoiding credit default have not yielded dividends to these borrowers in terms of development finance. Indeed, as the process continues, a shadow of debt overhang dampens the prospects of securing external finance for development. A mounting debt, combined with risks of default, has dissuaded potential creditors from offering more credits to these countries.

This chapter questions the mandates of the Bretton Woods institutions (BWIs), focusing attention on the International Monetary Fund (IMF). Mandates which guided the functioning of these international financial institutions (IFIs) in the past clearly failed to arrest the current process of economic stagnation in the developing areas. Nor have private international credit agencies filled the gap in development finance, which is needed in addition to the requirements needed for debt financing.

Following this introduction, the next section draws attention to the fact that the disciplinary as well as the financing role of the IMF has had little to do with the rich industrialized member nations. The main thrust of its operations has been directed toward the developing country members. This is paradoxical in view of the fact that these nations currently have little access to resources advanced by the IMF. Estimates of Fund access facilities and their distribution among the industrial and the developing countries support this argument. Attention has been drawn to the ground rules for determining votes and access to Fund resources: both are proportional to the quotas held by the individual members. The practice speaks of the inequities of the Fund system, especially in the context of its major clients, which today comprise the debt-ridden developing economies.

Next, this chapter focuses on the debt-overhang scenario in the developing areas. It examines the adequacy of concerted lendings by private banks or official agencies, via debt forgiveness or the menu-based voluntary approaches. It then reviews the actual measures and proposals for debt repayment and redressal as described in the professional literature.

The last part of this chapter proposes global Keynesianism as a basis for a new IMF mandate. This proposal would be effective in regenerating the flow of international capital in the service of global growth and development. The proposed reforms could improve the balance between industry and finance in the advanced economies, reducing the present unhealthy and unsustainable dominance of finance.

THE IMF AND CURRENT INTERNATIONAL FINANCE

Since the mid-1970s the industrial economies have not relied on the IMF, neither in terms of its surveillance over their exchange rates or domestic economic policies nor by using Fund facilities. The major industrialized countries have moved the coordination of their economic policies from the IMF to the G–7 summit meetings. Moreover, with the deregulation and closer integration of the world's international capital markets, the flow of international capital between the industrial countries has increased dramatically. The G–7 countries' access limits to the Fund drawing rights were rendered redundant. Indeed, it is no longer a problem, even for the deficit countries like the United Kingdom or the United States to attract private international capital, as seen from the magnitude of the funds flowing into these countries during the 1980s. Thus, the Fund has ceased to have a functional role in relation to the major industrial member countries, in marked contrast to the continued dominance of these nations over the BWIs.

These tendencies mark a departure from the 1960s when Fund resources supported the US dollar and the British pound. A cursory glance at the data provided by the IMF's *International Financial Statistics* indicates that between 1967 and 1977, the industrial country members drew SDR 14.3 billions of Fund credit, which constituted 53.1 per cent of aggregate Fund drawings under the General Resources Account (GRA) of that period. In contrast, drawings by the industrial countries fell to SDR 0.7 billion between 1978 and 1992, a sum which was only 1.1 per cent of the entire GRA drawings during that period.

On the other hand, drawings by the developing countries under the GRA account rose from SDR 12.67 billion, or 46.7 per cent for the period of 1967–77, to SDR 68.61 billion or 98.9 per cent for the period of 1978–92. In addition, the developing countries also drew on other special Fund facilities like Structural Adjustment Facilities (SAFs), Enhanced Structural Adjustment Facilities (ESAFs) and Trust Funds, for which the sum moved up from SDR 0.15 billion (1962–77) to 5.98 billion (1978–92). The industrial countries never had any occasion to draw from any special Fund facilities.[1] Thus, the IMF's role of providing funds for balance-of-payments deficits is of less and less importance for the industrial countries, but of more and more importance for the developing countries.

The industrial countries hold the major share of quotas in terms of the IMF system since these quotas are based on national income and a few other macroeconomic variables, such as exchange reserves and the level of trade. Thus, quotas determine the relative status of individual members within the Fund. A larger quota holding qualified an individual member not only to a larger drawing facility but also to a more effective voting right (which is set in proportion to the quota size), including a possible veto on critical issues. The gap between the rich and the poor nations is thus transmitted to the operational rules of the Fund in terms of the privileges and power enjoyed by its members.[2]

In October 1993, the aggregate quotas stood at SDR 144.8 billion.[3] The industrialized nations, with SDR 88.42 billion, constituted 61.06 per cent of the total.[4] The United States alone commanded SDR 26.52 billion (or 18.31 per cent of the total).[5] Quota stocks held by the developing countries were naturally much smaller and the top 12 debtors (Argentina, Brazil, China, Egypt, India, Indonesia, Mexico, Nigeria, the Philippines, Poland, Turkey and Venezuela)[6] with the most acute need to utilize the quota-linked drawing facilities held only SDR 19.57 billion or 13.52 per cent of the total Fund quotas, less than what the United States has alone.

It is possible to calculate the percentage of cumulative access limits which define the rights of individual members in the Fund. On a cumulative basis, the limits of aggregate drawings (access limits) of a member's respective quota size is illustrated in Table 2.1.

Applying this limit of 745 per cent of aggregate drawings to the cumulative access limits of the Fund it is possible to calculate the limit of aggregate drawings in SDRs, which is demonstrated in Table 2.2 overleaf.

The aggregate quotas held by the members of the Fund increased from SDR 91.2 billion to SDR 144.8 billion in October 1993 as a consequence of the Ninth General Review of Quotas in June 1990. It was specified, however, that 'no member's quota could be increased unless members having at least a specified percentage – 85 per cent until December 31, 1991 and 70 per cent thereafter – of total IMF quotas as of May 30, 1990, had consented to their increases in quotas'.[7]

A sub-group of members, all of whom were rich industrialized countries, retained veto power over important matters like quota revisions. Between them, they held a major portion of the quota. The June 1990 review of quotas also provided a suspension of voting and other rights (including the quota enhancements) if an individual member did not consent to, or

Table 2.1:
Limits of Aggregate Drawings (in percentage of country quota)

1. Reserve Tranche	up to 25%
2. Stand-By and Extended Arrangements	up to 300%
3. Special Facilities:	
a. Compensatory and Contingency Financing Facility	up to 95%
b. Buffer Stock Financing Facility	up to 35%
c. Systematic Transformation Facility	up to 50%
4. Structural Adjustment Facility	up to 50%
5. Enhanced Structural Adjustment Facility	up to 190%
Sum of 1–5:	up to 745%

Source: *IMF Survey*, Supplement on the IMF, October 1993, p. 22.

Table 2.2: Limits of Aggregate Drawings (in SDRs)

Industrialized countries:

France	SDR 55.24 billion
Germany	SDR 61.40 billion
Japan	SDR 61.40 billion
United Kingdom	SDR 55.24 billion
United States	SDR 162.97 billion
G–7 countries	SDR 462.64 billion
Sum of industrialized countries	SDR 658.73 billion

Debtor Countries:

Argentina	SDR 11.45 billion
Brazil	SDR 16.17 billion
China	SDR 25.22 billion
India	SDR 22.76 billion
Mexico	SDR 13.06 billion
Venezuela	SDR 14.54 billion
Top 12 debtor countries	SDR 145.80 billion

Access limit for all members	SDR 1,078.76 billion

Source: Own calculations based on quotas as of October 13, 1993, printed in *IMF Survey*, Supplement on the IMF, October 1993, p. 7.

failed to meet, the enhanced liabilities of the Fund in terms of the quota increases. It is revealing that as of October 13, 1993, 10 IMF members (Haiti, Iraq, Lebanon, Liberia, Sierra Leone, Somalia, Sudan, Tajikistan, Zaire and Zambia) had not yet paid their quota increases under the Ninth General Review of Quotas.[8]

Inequities in IMF governance over its facilities have caused serious shortcomings, notably, inadequate Fund resources to resolve the debt-overhang in the developing countries. Since a major part of Fund quotas is held by the industrialized countries – who no longer need to use such quotas – the possible aggregate Fund drawings (of SDR 882.06 billion for April 1993) are grossly under-utilized. The persistent resistance by some industrial nations to upward quota revisions and to create additional SDRs prevails in Fund deliberations – an attitude originating in the formative stages of the Bretton Woods institutions. Keynes' proposals for an International Clearing Union,[9] if implemented, probably would have kept in check the conservative and deflationary stance of the IMF, which had degenerated into monetarism by the end of the 1960s.[10]

As calculated in Table 2.2, in October 1993, the access limits to Fund drawing facilities were only SDR 145.80 billion for the top 12 debtors. This sum was less than one-eighth of their total external debt, then amounting to SDR 1170.5 billion by the end of 1992.

Total debt service payments (that is, repayments on principal and interest payments) for the developing countries as a whole were US$179 billion (SDR 127.8 billion) in 1992. This compared unfavorably with new disbursements of only US$167 billion (SDR 119 billion) during 1992. The amount of net flows on debts (that is, new disbursements minus principal repayments) from all the IFIs was a meager US$12.7 billion (SDR 9.0 billion). This sum included concessional funds from the International Development Association (IDA) as well as nonconcessional loans from the World Bank, the IMF and regional development banks.[11]

In practice, the IFIs actually generated very little liquidity for the purpose of debt servicing on a net basis. One needs to recall that IMF and World Bank credits were, with the exception of IDA credits, on a short- to medium-term basis. This ruled out additions to the net flows, even when gross disbursements were large. In reality, access to BWI resources was inadequate compared to the annual debt-service liabilities of the developing countries. Finally, all these flows were debt-creating, thus implying heavy flows of annual liabilities during the medium and the short run. The question of reducing, let alone eliminating, the debt overhang by means of inflows of funds, is thus ruled out. Moreover, most BWI funds were usually matched by high conditionality, tying debtor countries' balance-of-payments adjustments to a package of deflationary economic policies.

Arguments, offered within Fund-Bank circles, that the BWIs would eventually instil higher growth rates in the developing areas, have been based on the assumption that there would be long-term efficiency gains through price stabilization which would result in increased production and increased private credit from the international market. However, not many of these benefits have actually taken place since the developing countries are still struggling against debt overhang and the impeded development process.

DEBT OVERHANG AND DEBT MANAGEMENT

Groups Concerned with Developing Country Debt

Debt owed by the developing countries which, until recently, occupied the center stage of policy discussions on international finance, has generally been of concern to three distinct groups. Each group has a stake in how the debt problem has been managed since its flare-up in 1982. The three groups are private credit agencies of the lending countries, official bilateral and multilateral credit agencies and developing-country borrowers.

The private credit agencies in the lending countries have been the most active in debt negotiations, in terms of both the profitability of their current operations and the asset values based on past operations. The official bilateral and multilateral credit agencies have been trying to ease the debt situation in a bid to safeguard the interests not only of the different sectors in the lender economies but also those of the borrowing economies. The developing-country governments, which guarantee the private as well as public borrowings of the developing countries, remain the least vocal group in the debt negotiation process.

For a lender agency bent on profit maximization, it is crucial to maintain a net outflow of finance while simultaneously preventing all possible lapses of returns on past net outflows. At a macroeconomic level, a creditor country's strategy to maintain a net outflow helps to maintain a macroeconomic balance between savings and investment in the domestic economy. Maintaining net outflows of finance also ensures a current account surplus (net of interest receipts from abroad) and hence an export surplus in commodities and services other than interest payments. Given the possibility that capital exports from a lending country are capable of generating current account earnings – both as net export earnings on goods and as net investment income from past investments – one can draw a distinction between the 'trade effect' of capital exports (which consists of the net export generating effects) and the '*rentier* effect' (operating via net investment income inflows). For a given rate of growth for capital exports, there is a potential conflict between the trader interest and the *rentier* interest in lending countries.[12]

It is useful, at this stage, to draw a distinction between borrowing countries from developing areas and those from the industrial areas. Imports of the first group largely consist of commodities rather than services (which exclude debt servicing). Further, the second group imports more services and less commodities. Allocation of the gross flow of credit between the two groups of borrowing countries is thus important in determining whether the *rentier* or the trader interests would be served by capital exports in the lending country. The positive trade effect in the lending country has its counterpart in the developing country in terms of a real transfer of resources from abroad. The latter provides a mirror image in the developing region where domestic growth is dependent, other factors remaining the same, on net inflow of financial (and hence real) resources. One should not miss the mutual interest between the trader interests in the lending areas and the developing countries offering potential markets for commodity exports from the lending areas. Evidently a larger flow of net financial resources in the direction of the developing countries makes up the case for global Keynesianism, generating demand for real transactions in the world as a whole.

Contrary to what is warranted by such common goals of the lender and debtor countries, actual policies implemented to manage developing-country debt have been in the interest of finance, represented by banks, security houses and related institutions which promote what is defined here as *rentier* interest.

Debt Reduction Policy Approaches

Analysts of developing-country debt policies distinguish among the three prevailing approaches to the debt issue:

- outright debt forgiveness,

- concerted lendings on the part of official and private credit agencies and

- menu-based voluntary reductions of privately held debt, which depend on debt instruments like securitization, market-based sales and equity swaps, and bond-financed debt buy-backs.

Arguments favoring outright debt forgiveness or concerted lending by the creditor agencies follow a logic which is somewhat as follows: debt stock held by a borrowing country, beyond a ceiling, would prove to be counter-productive not only for the debtors but also for the creditors, since creditors risk a potential drop in the discounted market value of their developing-country debt-related assets to levels where further debts reduce the aggregate discounted value of debt held. In such circumstances, the creditors are prompted to forgive part of the debt or to provide refinancing in a concerted lending. Thus, concerted lendings by official and private credit agencies aim to avoid debt defaults by maintaining the flow of debt services. Little money was left over from these concerted lendings for development after meeting the debt charges.

While debtor nations prefer debt forgiveness, creditors lose any future claim on the forgiven debt if the economic situation of the debtor countries improves. Creditors have thus preferred concerted lending rather than loan forgiveness. In the event of actual losses from developing-country loans, the major private banks, who have already secured loan loss provisionings, do not face problems.

By the late 1980s, there were widespread tendencies to use menu-based voluntary reductions of privately held debt through debt instruments like securitization, market-based sales and equity swaps. Nicholas Brady, US Treasury Secretary, was the leading force in institutionalizing these instruments through the 1989 Brady Plan. However, the menu approach has had little impact on developing-country debt.

The logic of developing-country debt management policy, using market-based menu options with concerted lending, is beset with free-rider problems. Attempts to sell additional debt at discounts are fraught with the danger of a downward slide in the average market value of the debt stock. Efforts by official bilateral or multilateral creditors to forestall declines in debt prices by guaranteeing debtor-country bonds (which are issued to buy back their own debt) may work as long as the new bonds carry sufficient confidence in the market. (Holding a $100 debt stock with 50 per cent discount would not change the debtor's portfolio if bought back with cash from bonds issued – the discount on which is the same.)

With most debtors, the support available from creditor governments or the IFIs has so far been too thin to have significant impact on bond-financed debt buy-backs.[13] Buy-backs financed by debtor governments are similarly difficult. It is unrealistic to think that the debt-ridden nations with their sparse exchange reserves are able to use these reserves for buy-backs. Swaps, between debt and debtor-country equities, also face additional hurdles, including the non-availability of equities with good international credit ratings and potential inflationary consequences in debtor economies.

Very little of the developing country debt was reduced by the different official and private actions since 1985 when debt conversion programs caught on. The cumulative sum of debt conversion implemented between 1985 and 1992 amounted to $72.99 billion or SDR 51.40 billion. The major form of debt conversions consisted of debt-equity swaps and debt buy-backs. The effect of debt conversions, at an aggregate sum of SDR 51.40 billion, was too little in terms of the total debt service (TDS) of SDR 125.69 billion and external debt stock (EDT) of SDR 1170.5 billion, by the end of 1992.[14]

Debt-Reduction Proposals

At the beginning of 1982, when Mexico was near default, the private banks with high exposures sought some prudential or regulatory supervision. In 1983, the monetary authorities of the United States approved an International Lending Supervisory Act (ILSA). The act made use of the prevailing '90-days non-accrual asset rule', that is, interest-earning assets were rendered non-performing if unpaid for more than 90 days.

A steering committee, which was led by nine US money center banks, suggested involuntary bank lendings to borrowers who were approved by the IMF on a strict case-by-case basis. Simultaneously, pre-payments by any debtor were to be shared by all creditor banks, ruling out inter-bank rivalry in receiving payments.[15] In effect the ILSA introduced a creditor's cartel, one where the individual debtor had little scope to negotiate with the respective creditor at a direct level. Simultaneously the move warded off the threats of an immediate debt collapse, an outcome welcomed by the creditor banks.

Concerted lendings, backed by case-by-case negotiations between banks, the IMF and the developing country debtors, were inadequate. Therefore, in October 1985, James A. Baker, then US Secretary of Treasury, launched a proposal to resume new loans to the 15 most heavily indebted countries, including 10 from Latin America. The plan was inadequate to tackle the $420.4 billion debt held by the highly indebted countries by the end of 1985.[16]

However, by the time the Baker Plan ended in 1988, debt held by the developing countries had already fallen considerably. Thus private bank claims on Latin America and Sub-

Saharan Africa fell by $15 billion during 1985–88. The decline continued over the next few years. But, despite the Baker Plan's promises, voluntary bank lendings were not forthcoming even to debtors willing to follow suggested changes in economic policies.[17]

On a closer look a major factor explaining the steady reductions in the stock of outstanding debt during the late 1980s was a tapering-off in the gross as well as net flows of developing-country credit. Thus swaps (which amounted to a mere $16 billion) and new money advanced by the banks (another $13 billion) during the second half of the 1980s could not explain the declines in the debt stock during the period.[18]

Confidentiality in terms of possible loan losses of the creditor banks was considered important in order to avoid erosion of investors' confidence in bank stocks. Interestingly, with banks of different national origins controlling the international credit market, average bank profitability was also viewed as an index of a creditor nation's financial standing. This is related to the use of provisionings, which have been popular among banks as a tool of debt-management policy.[19]

By 1989, when the US Secretary of Treasury, Nicholas Brady, launched a drive to initiate a voluntary and menu-driven option for the banks, the major US banks had already unloaded substantial stocks of developing-country debt in the market. For example, Citicorp's exposure to developing-country debtors was cut by $1.2 billion in 1988.[20] The market value of a dollar debt was around 67 cents during 1988.[21] According to the estimates provided by the *Wall Street Journal*, trade in debt was at $15 billion for 1988.[22] The World Bank has put the total volume of turnover on the secondary debt market at $50 billion for 1988 and $60–80 billion for 1989.

As pointed out by Salomon Brothers, the demand from multinational corporations and from official agencies for debt-equity swaps and direct buy-backs at a discount did not reverse the stagnating demand for debt which in 1988 was at its overall record low at 20 cents and in 1989 at 11.5 cents in Argentina. In general, risky trade of debt securities and a low spread caused a low dealer profile in the secondary market for developing-country debt.[23] Debt buy-backs had only limited success because of two reasons: (a) they usually increased the value of the remaining debt[24] and thus helped banks which kept back debts, and (b) the volume of debt sales has proven to be unsatisfactory, especially for large banks which generally held a large volume of debt.

Simultaneously, the falling debt prices in the market indicated the inadequacy of the device to elevate adequate demand for these instruments in the market. Sometimes negative pledges in the syndicated loan agreements discouraged sales of these assets to third parties. Examples include the cross-default clause (allowing the same rights to all creditors during a debt crisis) and mandatory repayment.[25]

Brady's plan to seek support from the IMF and the World Bank in resolving the debt issue followed from his earlier testimony in the US Senate 'to keep US leadership in debt-related issues'.[26] The plan met with limited success in terms of private banks lending more to Fund-Bank approved clients. On the other side, only five of the 15 highly indebted countries (HICs) could actually take advantage of the plan. On the whole, the G–10 nations, other than the United States, had reservations about providing what they thought 'smacks of subsidy' especially with the Fund's encouragement to lend into arrears.[27] An appeal by the Interim Committee of the Fund to the banks for 'new money' to the Brady Plan borrowers had little support from private bankers. Even private agencies like Moody's Investor Service criticized the World Bank guarantees as 'legitimized forgiveness to debtor governments'.[28]

In March 1989, Japan, which had the highest developing-country exposure ($80 billion), made its participation in the Brady Plan conditional on the fulfillment of the other parties' quotas (including private banks, governments and IFIs).[29] The Brady Plan, in fact, opened a whole Pandora's box by admitting officially that the developing countries could never pay back their loans. Consistent with this position, the United States for the first time agreed to a cutback, though only a fringe, of the developing-country debt. On the whole, the under-funded Brady Plan, as well as the dampened secondary market for debt, were pointers for private creditors that it was no longer profitable to lend to the developing borrowers.

It is now logical to turn to the non-banking assets which, by the early 1990s, had effectively replaced the developing-country debt in bank portfolios. As the distance between banks and security houses narrowed in the market, securities proved more important as sources of bank earnings. However, the wide-ranging securitizations made banks more vulnerable to market risks, a problem which was difficult to mend by means of prudential legislation.[30] According to the Bank for International Settlement (BIS), the stock of bank assets with non-banks was at $1851.4 billion by the end of

1991. The sum was substantial, compared to the total stock of bank assets with banks and non-banks at $7492.2 billion at the end of 1991. Similarly, liabilities of banks at the end of 1991 were at $7358.7 billion and the sum with non-banks was $1264.4 billion.[31]

As a consequence, the non-interest income of banks as a percentage of their income was 41.1 per cent for the United Kingdom and 38.8 per cent for the United States during 1990. For Japan, Germany and France the respective percentages were 35.9 per cent, 34.9 per cent, and 24.9 per cent.[32] Proposals for debt management from different quarters include suggestions such as a global debt relief. This has been advanced, for example, by US Senator Bradley who in 1986 sought debt redressal by means of reductions in interest rates and repayments phased over a period of three years. Trade expansions likely to result from the reorganization of debtor economies formed a major plank of the mutual gain envisaged in that plan. In a similar proposal, Harvard economist Jeffrey Sachs sought a relief of interest payments for countries with heavy losses in income. However, the precondition for such a grant was a program of stabilization and reform.[33] Stanley Fischer[34] advocated a similar plan as did Argentina's President Alfonsin, who sought World Bank co-financing. In another and rather extreme suggestion, the President of Peru, Alan Garcia, sought unilateral debtor action by limiting debt servicing to a maximum of 20 per cent of a country's export earnings. Interestingly, MIT economist Paul Krugman supported linking debt servicing to the 'state of nature' faced by the debtor countries which include the external environment, the export prospects and interest rates on outstanding debt.[35]

Debt relief has also been sought through portfolio adjustments. Rohatyn and Kenen[36] suggested creating a separate fund for an International Debt Facility (IDF). Various proposals, including one for an International Debt Discount Facility (IDDF) by Peter Kenen,[37] seek the support of creditor governments and the IFIs to settle and liquidate the debt accumulated by the developing countries. Practical difficulties of implementing the scheme evoked suggestions to help raise resources. These ideas included Cooper's suggestion to sell the IMF's gold stock at market prices,[38] and the United Nations Conference on Trade and Development's (UNCTAD)[39] suggestion for creditor-government vigilance over capital flight from the developing countries since funds are deposited in creditor-countries' private banks.

Davidson, Dore and Tarshis have advanced schemes of debt relief which are similar in spirit.[40] They agree that debt service, in Keynes' words,[41] has become an annual tribute, constituting a serious impediment to world trade and income, threatening the stability of international payments. Originally proposed by Tarshis,[42] Davidson invokes the intervention of industrialized countries' central banks in relieving the developing-country debt stock.[43] A similar stand was taken earlier by Eaton, Gersovitz and Stiglitz[44] in identifying the debt problem as an application of moral hazard – a situation in which the overall optimal solution can only be provided by outside intervention. In other words, the debt problem is an application of the typical prisoner's dilemma, that is, a situation where the impossibility of coordinating responses leads to inferior results, which could be prevented if coordination were possible. Tarshis' proposal involved the central bank of the creditor nation purchasing a stipulated portion of debt held by commercial banks at a discount and on a gradual basis. The banks would deposit proceeds of the debt sale with the central bank. Then, the central bank could cancel the debt in a manner suitable. Some positive aspects of the proposal include:

- it avoids a 'free rider' issue, since all banks within the jurisdiction of the corresponding central bank have the same right;

- the private loss from discounts on developing-country debt held by commercial banks is socially recognized by central banks as they try to avoid bank bankruptcies and as they reduce the possibility of debt hampering the growth in international trade; and

- there are no direct fiscal side-effects on industrialized country governments since they are not required to absorb the losses.

While in Davidson's proposal the central banks sell stocks or loan securities to the governments in exchange for government bonds and the governments ultimately negotiate a forgiveness ratio with individual debtors, the Tarshis proposal entrusts the central bank with the entire process. This later proposal avoids the fiscal problems of a debt held by the creditors' governments. Moreover, the Tarshis proposal avoids problems based on the geopolitical basis of debt negotiations.

Despite all these proposals, the debt issue has remained as unresolved and sensitive as it was in the early 1980s. Questions of propriety have constrained even the most benevolent industrial country governments because of the tax-paying public's resistance to outright debt forgiveness or wide-ranging concessions. Nor have the banks favored such proposals, not even when money was forthcoming from public sources. They feared the possible dampening impact of such transactions on the market value of bank assets held in the form of developing-country debt.

Proposals to involve the IFIs on a larger scale in debt reduction have also remained remote; IFI debt management had more to do with debt financing than debt reduction. The small sum of money lent by the IFIs on a net basis was conditioned on debtors' domestic adjustments. The overall impact of these adjustments has been regressive and contractionary for the world economy: 'To foster deflationary policies on the deficit countries will merely unleash global recessionary economic forces making both creditor and debtor nations economically worse off.'[45]

PLEA FOR A GLOBAL KEYNESIAN APPROACH: REFORM OF THE IMF

It is in the mutual interest of both industrialized and developing nations that the world economy expand as a whole. Such expansions, combined with a dismantling of trade restrictions, would considerably enlarge the markets for goods produced in the North and the South.

The recent spurt in international private capital flows, especially in the securitized sector, has remained confined to the industrially advanced economies. External bond offerings amounted to $333.7 billion in 1992, recording an annual percentage increase of 47 per cent over the $227.1 billion bond offerings during 1988. The industrialized countries received about 95 per cent of the total external bond offerings in 1992. Even syndicated bank credits, which amounted to only $117.9 billion in 1992, went primarily to the industrial countries, which received 88 per cent of the total.[46]

These movements in international capital have failed to generate real growth and employment in the industrial economies. For example, for 1991, real growth has been at about 1 per cent in the G–7 and only 0.5 per cent in the other industrial countries. For the 1980s as a whole the growth rate for the G–7 was 3 per cent and for the other industrial countries only 2.7 per cent. Similarly, the developing countries have been maintaining a real growth rate between 3 and 4 per cent during the 1980s and a real growth rate of 3.5 per cent for 1991. This performance was only marginally superior to the industrialized countries. In the developing regions, growth in Latin America, which includes the major debtors, had been particularly low with the growth rate of 0.1 per cent (1988), 1.6 per cent (1989), 1.4 per cent (1990) and 2.2 per (1991).[47]

Paradoxes of booming finance in the industrial economies, which otherwise were nearly stagnant in terms of growth in real output, can be explained by the dissociation of financial from real transactions. The boom in finance, which accommodated both domestic and international capital, was based on uncertainty-related speculation in these economies. Growth in financial and other services, which similarly flourished in these economies, generated a climate of instability and financial fragility. Frequent runs on stock exchanges and fluctuations in interest rates and exchange rates in these countries symbolized such instabilities.

Consistent with earlier observations that trade among the industrial countries consisted more of services than of manufactured goods was the disproportionate growth of the service sector in these otherwise stagnant economies. In contrast, the developing countries have remained net purchasers of commodities (including manufactures). This fact illustrates the potential for generating new markets for industrial products in developing countries by diverting net flows of finance toward debtor countries.[48]

Renewed flows of net finance from abroad could generate new demand for goods (rather than services) if the developing countries were the major recipients.

Considering the expansionary effects of these financial flows for both developing and industrial countries, the case is made for ending debt overhang by both official and private credit agencies in the industrial areas. The limited and contractionary impact of the IFIs on debt-redressal mechanisms calls for the IMF especially to rethink possible reforms. Most of the quotas under the IMF are held by the industrial economies; about 43 per cent by the G–10 alone. Since quota-linked Fund drawings are little used by industrial economies, Fund operations clearly generate a deflationary bias in the world economy. This is achieved both by disciplining the developing borrowers to a path of deflationary adjustment and by keeping dormant the credit lines (access limits) earmarked for the industrial-country members who control a major part of such facilities.

A new International Debt Facility (IDF) should be established. Phased utilization and compulsory release of the Fund access limits held by industrial countries could provide needed resources. A major part of these drawings would be under reserve and first credit tranche, both of which are unconditional. This would release funds for the IDF which could be collectively or individually operated by the industrial countries. Compared to the alternative proposals for debt relief, for example, Kenen's proposal for an International Debt Discount Facility (IDDF), the proposal could be financed and managed without being questioned by tax-payers in rich countries. Simultaneously, it would correct the imbalances and inequities within the present Fund system by indirectly permitting the developing countries to use more of the Fund's access facilities.

The proposal would reduce the current deflationary stance of the IMF because sources of concessionary credit would not be required. With funds released by the IMF, the surplus industrial nations may even be persuaded to adopt expansionary policies while countries with weak balance of payments (for example, the United States or the United Kingdom) could use these financial resources toward expansionary policies. The Fund should seek to implement policies in these industrial countries which, like the policies associated with Structural Adjustment Facilities (SAFs) in developing countries, would open up the domestic markets of the industrial countries as well. As a special concession, those countries which release such funds may be exempted from their responsibilities in terms of the concessional development assistance. Hopefully, this would not shrink the aggregate size of such concessionary aid available to the developing countries.

Finally, as a reciprocal concession, the developing countries may be persuaded to make sure that the money released by the IDF for debt cancellation leads to an expansion of expenditures in these countries which have a social orientation. A great degree of compliance on the part of the industrial nations and an active, non-discriminatory policy on the part of the IMF would go a long way to restore and revive the growth potentials of the world as a whole. This would put an end to the current zero-sum strategies of the powerful creditors by making debt policies redundant in an expansionary world.

Notes

1. International Monetary Fund, *International Financial Statistics*, Year Book 1992 (Washington, D.C.: International Monetary Fund, 1992).
2. According to Sir Hans W. Singer, the main reason the financially

powerful countries have shifted their support to the Bretton Woods system while their support to the UN system has been eroded, lies in the different voting methods governing the two systems. The Bretton Woods system is essentially based on the principle of one dollar one vote; that is, voting proportionate to financial support, whereas the UN system is based on one country one vote. This latter voting method gives the financially powerful countries control of the BWIs which they therefore consider their own. Statement made by Sir Hans W. Singer at the World Hearings on Development, Theme 5, United Nations, New York, on June 10, 1994 (afternoon session).

3. See *IMF Survey*, Supplement on the IMF, October 1993, p. 1.
4. Calculated from Quotas as printed in *IMF Survey*, Supplement on the IMF, October 1993, p. 7.
5. See *IMF Survey*, Supplement on the IMF, October 1993, Table of p. 7.
6. As listed in Table 21 of the World Bank's *World Development Report 1993* (Washington, DC: World Bank, 1993) pp. 278–9.
7. *IMF Survey*, Supplement on the IMF, October 1993, p. 8, column 1.
8. See *IMF Survey*, Supplement on the IMF, October 1993, footnote 1 of Table on p. 7.
9. See John Maynard Keynes, *Proposals for an International Clearing Union*, British Government Publication No. 6437 (London: HMSO, 1943).
10. As noted by Paul Davidson, the international debt crisis of the 1980s would never have occurred if the Keynes proposal for the post-World War II international monetary system had been adopted: Paul Davidson, 'A Modest Set of Proposals for Resolving the International Debt Problem' in *Journal of Post-Keynesian Economics*, vol. 10/2 (Winter 1987/88) p. 329. Moreover, Hans W. Singer noted at the SID World Conference, Mexico, in April 1994 that what can be learned from Keynes is that the best way of tackling surpluses is not to eliminate them by deflationary actions and reactions. Instead, the rational way is to use these surpluses for expansionist policies in the service of full employment and the fulfillment of agreed international purposes. Keynes also foresaw and emphasized the dangers of a debt trap which consists of a vicious circle under which the pressure to service debts increases the export pressures among the debtor countries which in turn worsen their terms of trade, which in turn makes it all the more difficult to repay the debts. Keynes developed these views after the First World War in his book *The Economic Consequences of the Peace* in connection with the problem of the German reparations, when he formulated the concept of an additional transfer burden of a debtor country.
11. World Bank, *World Debt Tables 1994–95*, Volume I (Washington, DC: World Bank, 1994) pp. 7 and 192. The amounts in SDR are calculated with the 1992 average exchange rate of US$1.40 per SDR.

12. For an analysis more detailed than the verbal explanation given here and in the next paragraphs, see Sunanda Sen, 'Swings and Paradoxes in International Capital Markets: A Theoretical Note' in *Cambridge Journal of Economics*, vol. 15/2 (June 1991) pp. 179–98 and Sunanda Sen, 'Dimensions of India's External Crisis' in *Economic and Political Weekly*, vol. 29/14 (April 2, 1994) pp. 805–12.

13. Bolivia is one of the exceptions, where support from creditor countries and the World Bank had an impact on bond-financed debt buy-backs.

14. World Bank, *World Debt Tables 1992–93* (Washington, DC: World Bank, 1992).

15. See Ennio Rodriguez and Stephany Griffith-Jones, *Cross-Conditionality, Banking Regulations and Third World Debt: The Experiences of Chile and Mexico* (Basingstoke, Hampshire, England: Macmillan, 1991) p. 17.

16. Hossein Askari, *The Foreign Debt: National Development Conflict* (New York: Quorum Books, 1986) p. 17.

17. Richard N. Cooper, *Economic Stabilization and Debt in Developing Countries* (Cambridge, MA: MIT Press, 1992) p. 152.

18. World Bank, *World Debt Tables* (1992–93).

19. This was especially the case in continental Europe where governments tacitly accepted hidden bank reserves, which often consisted of provisionings. By the mid-1980s provisionings had spread rather widely, covering the United Kingdom as well as the United States. As financial deregulation began to challenge banks in the United Kingdom and the United States, these banks followed the practice of Japanese banks in choosing securities as the main form of assets in their portfolios.

20. *Financial Times* of January 18, 1989.

21. 'Indecent Exposures' in *Financial Times* of January 31, 1987.

22. Hossein Askari, *Third World Debt and Financial Innovations: The Experiences of Chile and Mexico* (Paris: OECD, 1991) p. 38.

23. *Financial Times* of December 19, 1989.

24. Michael P. Dooley, 'Buy-Backs and the Market Valuation of External Debt' in *IMF Staff Papers*, vol. 35/2 (June 1988) pp. 215–29.

25. Askari, *The Foreign Debt*, pp. 67–8.

26. *Financial Times* of June 10, 1988.

27. *Financial Times* of April 10, 1989.

28. *Financial Times* of April 4, 1989.

29. *Financial Times* of March 17, 1989.

30. *Financial Times* of April 3, 1989.

31. Bank for International Settlements (BIS), *62nd Annual Report* (Basel, Switzerland: BIS, 1992).

32. Bank for International Settlement, *62nd Annual Report* (1992).

33. Jeffrey D. Sachs and Susan M. Collins, *Developing Country Debt and Economic Performance* (Chicago, IL: University of Chicago Press, 1989).

34. Stanley Fischer, Professor of Economics at MIT, is currently First Deputy Managing Director of the IMF. Before that, he was Chief Economist at the World Bank.

35. Paul Krugman, 'Financing vs Forgiving a Debt Overhang' in *Journal of Development Economics*, vol. 29/3 (November 1988) pp. 253–68.

36. Felix Rohatyn and Peter B. Kenen, *The Debt Crisis and the World Economy: Report by a Group of Commonwealth Experts* (London: Commonwealth Institute, 1984).

37. Peter B. Kenen, 'Organizing Debt Relief: The Need for a New Institution' in *Journal of Economic Perspectives*, vol. 4/1 (Winter 1990) pp. 7–18.

38. Richard N. Cooper, *Economic Stabilization and Debt in Developing Countries* (Cambridge, MA: MIT Press, 1992).

39. United Nations Conference on Trade and Development (UNCTAD), *Trade and Development Report 1988* (New York: United Nations, 1988).

40. Paul Davidson, 'A Modest Set of Proposals for Resolving the International Debt Problem' in *Journal of Post-Keynesian Economics*, vol. 10, no. 2 (Winter 1987/88) pp. 323–38; M.H.I. Dore and Lorie Tarshis, 'The LDC Debt and the Commercial Banks: A Proposed Solution' in *Journal of Post-Keynesian Economics*, vol. 12, no. 3 (Spring 1990) pp. 452–65; and Lorie Tarshis, 'Disarming the International Debt Bomb' in *Challenge*, vol. 30/2 (May–June 1987) pp. 18–23.

41. John Maynard Keynes, *The Economic Consequences of the Peace* (London: Macmillan, 1919), reprinted in *The Collected Writings of John Maynard Keynes* volume II (London: Macmillan, 1971).

42. Tarshis, 'Disarming the International Debt Bomb', pp. 18–23.

43. Davidson, 'A Modest Set of Proposals...', p. 337.

44. Jonathan Eaton, Mark Gersovitz and Joseph E. Stiglitz, 'The Pure Theory of Country Risk' in *European Economic Review*, vol. 30 (June 1986) pp. 481–513.

45. Davidson, 'A Modest Set of Proposals...', p. 328.

46. United Nations Conference on Trade and Development (UNCTAD), *Trade and Development Report 1993* (New York: United Nations, 1993) p. 50.

47. Bank for International Settlement, *62nd Annual Report*.

48. Sen (1991) and Sunanda Sen, 'Financial Fragility and its World Implications' (mimeo, 1992).

3 Globalization of Financial Markets and Impact on Flows to LDCs: New Challenges for Regulation*

Stephany Griffith-Jones with Vassilis Papageorgiou[1]

INTRODUCTION

This chapter begins by describing recent trends in private financial markets, both globally and in less developed countries (LDCs). Analyses of the structural changes that have occurred in global private financial markets – particularly resulting from deregulation and liberalization – and attempts to evaluate their benefits and costs follow. Based on this analysis, an attempt is made to define the increase – and change in the nature – of risk, particularly of a systemic type. Special reference is made to risks as they affect LDCs. The chapter then reviews some of the main aspects of the supervisory and regulatory response to the changes in financial flows and, above all, to changes in perceived risk which they generate. Finally, conclusions are drawn and policy recommendations made, from those which are fairly widely accepted (but not implemented) to those which would be more innovative.

---

* Reprinted (with minor changes) from Jan Joost Teunissen (ed.), *The Pursuit of Reform: Global Finance and the Developing Countries* (The Hague, The Netherlands: Forum on Debt and Development (FONDAD), 1994).

RECENT TRENDS IN PRIVATE FINANCIAL MARKETS
AND IN FLOWS TO DEVELOPING COUNTRIES

Globally, in 1992, borrowing on international capital markets continued its rapid increase for the second year in a row. In 1991, there had been a rapid increase (of 20.7 per cent) in the aggregate volume of international capital flows; in 1992, there was a further increase of 16.2 per cent (see Table 3.1). In fact, in 1992, global borrowing was at a level 54 per cent above its 1987 level.

Though borrowing on international capital markets by developing countries continued to increase in 1992 to the highest level since the early 1980s, the growth (at 2.3 per cent) was negligible in real terms, according to estimates of the Organization for Economic Cooperation and Development (OECD). It was also *far lower* than growth in 1991, when developing countries were reported to have had an increase of 62 per cent in the volume of borrowing on international capital markets, from $28.6 billion to $46.2 billion (see again Table 3.1). In comparison with the 1987 level, developing-countries' borrowing was 80 per cent above its 1987 level. Thus, growth of lending to LDCs has been faster over the 1987–92 period than that of global flows.

The total share of LDCs' borrowing first fell from 6.6 per cent in 1987 to 4.7 per cent in 1989, increased to 6.6 per cent in

Table 3.1
Borrowing on International Capital Markets (US$b)
(borrower composition)

Borrower	1987	1988	1989	1990	1991	1992
OECD countries	349.6	413.8	426.5	384.4	457.9	535.7
Developing countries	26.3	22.5	21.8	28.6	46.2	47.3
Eastern Europe	3.7	4.6	4.7	4.6	1.8	1.5
Others	13.3	12.6	13.5	17.3	19.0	25.2
Total	392.9	453.5	466.5	434.9	524.9	609.7
Year-on-year percentage change		15.7%	2.8%	–6.8%	20.7%	16.2%

Source: Organization for Economic Cooperation and Development (OECD), *Financial Market Trends*, vol. 54 (February 1993) p. 7.

1990, increased further to about 9 per cent in 1991, but declined somewhat in 1992. Indeed, it was growth in OECD countries' borrowing which accounted for practically all the rapid growth of global borrowing in 1992, whereas in 1991, LDC borrowing had contributed fairly significantly to that growth.

As in previous years, the main dynamism globally in 1992 did not come from syndicated loans (which remained at approximately the same level as in 1991), but came from growth of securities and non-underwritten facilities (see Table 3.2).

As can be seen from comparing Tables 3.2 and 3.3, developing countries seem to follow trends similar to global ones, with declining importance of syndicated loans (especially marked in 1992) and with sharp increases in securities, particularly important in 1992 in bonds, but also reflecting a continued large increase in equities. It is also noteworthy that non-underwritten facilities (which include Euro-commercial papers) increased a great deal in 1992, reaching the same level as equities.

According to other sources, such as the World Bank,[2] which has made major efforts to have complete coverage of these new flows to developing countries, the figures for private portfolio flows to LDCs are somewhat higher. Thus, according to World Bank recent estimates,[3] gross private portfolio flows to developing countries have grown explosively since 1989. Indeed, these flows, which averaged under $6 billion a year in the 1982–88 period, were estimated by the World Bank to have grown to an estimated $34 billion in 1992.

Table 3.2
Borrowing of the International Capital Markets (in US$b)

	1988	1989	1990	1991	1992
Securities	234.8	263.8	237.2	321.0	357.2
Loans	125.5	121.1	124.5	116.0	117.9
Committed back-up facilities	16.6	8.4	7.0	7.7	6.7
Non-underwritten facilities (incl. Euro-commercial papers)	76.6	73.2	66.2	80.2	127.9
Total	453.5	466.5	434.9	524.9	609.7
Year-on-year percentage change	+15.4	+2.8	-6.8	+20.7	+16.2

Source: OECD, *Financial Market Trends*, vol. 54 (February 1993) p. 87.

Table 3.3
Borrowing by Developing Countries (OECD definition)(in US$b)

Instruments	1987	1988	1989	1990	1991	1992
Bonds	3.1	4.2	2.6	4.5	8.3	14.0
Equities	0.0	0.3	0.1	1.0	5.0	7.2
Syndicated loans	20.1	17.4	16.2	19.8	26.7	16.5
Committed borrowing facilities	1.3	1.3	0.9	2.1	4.5	1.3
Non-underwritten facilities (inc. Euro-commercial papers)	1.8	1.2	2.0	1.2	1.7	7.9
Total	26.3	22.5	21.8	28.6	46.2	47.3

Source: OECD, *Financial Market Trends*, vol. 54 (February 1993), Statistical Annex.

The increase has reportedly gone largely to a few countries in Latin America, where gross equity flows have grown more than tenfold in four years, mainly via American Depositary Receipts (ADRs) and Global Depositary Receipts (GDRs), from $434 million in 1989 to an estimated $5.6 billion, and where bond financing increased almost fifteen-fold, from $833 million in 1989 to $11.7 billion in 1992 (see Table 3.4 overleaf).

Though the increase in securities flows to developing countries (and especially to Latin America) has been impressive, some analysts argue that these levels could be sustained or even increased, at least until the end of the century.[4] These kind of 'optimistic' estimates are based on very aggregate projections and draw on facts like:

- the sum of assets of pension funds, life insurance funds, mutual funds and others reach as much as $14 trillion;

- the share of their assets invested in developing-country stock markets is on average less than 5 per cent of foreign equity holdings, and less than 0.25 per cent of their total assets;

- an increase in the share of industrial countries' institutional

Table 3.4
Portfolio Investment in Latin America, 1989–92
(World Bank staff estimates in US$m)

Type of Investment	1989	1990	1991	1992
Equity investment from abroad of which	434	1,099	6,228	5,570
Closed-end funds	416	575	771	293
ADRs/GDRs	–	98	4,697	4,377
Direct equity investment	18	426	760	900
Bonds	833	2,673	6,848	11,732
Commercial paper	127	0	1,212	840
Certificates of deposit	0	0	670	1,100
Total	1,394	3,772	14,958	19,243

Source: World Bank, *Global Economic Prospects and the Developing Countries* (Washington, DC: World Bank, 1993) p. 36.

funds assets going to emerging markets from, for example, 0.25 per cent to 0.5 per cent could imply large increases of investments in those markets.

Similarly, it is also stressed that emerging stock-market capitalization represented 6 per cent of the world share of equity markets in 1991 (double its 1987 share, which is likely to increase). However, in coming years, there is considerable scope for international equity flows to LDCs if industrial-country investors hold developing-country stocks in proportion to the LDC market share in the global total.

Finally, though this chapter concentrates on borrowing, it is interesting to stress that foreign direct investment (FDI) flows to developing countries are estimated to have increased significantly in recent years, both in value (from $9.8 billion in 1986 to $35.9 billion in 1991) and as a share of global FDI (from 13 per cent in 1986 to 22 per cent in 1991).[5]

Though there may be specific causes encouraging FDI and lending flows to LDCs, the fact is that both FDI and lending flows to

LDCs are increasing in parallel. Roughly concentrating on the same region, it would seem to imply that similar underlying common causes (such as improved growth prospects in certain LDCs, recession in industrial countries) are also very important in explaining all these flows.

STRUCTURAL CHANGES IN GLOBAL PRIVATE FINANCIAL MARKETS

Deregulation and Financial Innovation

During the last ten years, the size and structure of financial markets have undergone profound changes. The process of structural change is very complex (largely because it is not homogeneous across countries), and is therefore difficult to understand at a global level. There are, however, many common features in the direction and in the key features of the changes, in most countries.

The dominant initial force explaining these changes is deregulation, which considerably enhanced the role of free-market forces in determining choices open to economic agents. By the beginning of the 1980s, many of the restrictions which previously limited competition (for example, restrictions on lines of businesses' geographical operation; quantitative restrictions on credit; interest rate and price restrictions; controls on foreign exchange transactions and international capital flows) had either been removed or else been undermined by market developments. As will be discussed below, in this context of much greater freedom, strengthening of capital adequacy standards became the main regulatory constraint on bank portfolio choices.

As a result, four trends have emerged. First, financial markets have become increasingly globalized and integrated. Domestic markets became progressively more integrated with each other and with offshore markets. Capital flows across borders intensified and the number of institutions operating in foreign centers increased. Furthermore, the global interlocking of national financial markets has far exceeded the global interlocking of national productive structures, as the very rapid growth of international financial flows was far quicker than the growth of trade and direct investment.

Second, the size and influence of markets on finance has increased markedly throughout all countries. Again, there is a con-

trast with the past, because until the end of the 1970s the importance of financial markets was more an Anglo-Saxon peculiarity.
Indeed, the fundamental changes in the regulatory and technological environment increased competitive pressures and – in a broadly
favorable macroeconomic environment – led to rapid growth in
financial activity and trading. The major expansion of the financial
industry world-wide (see Table 3.5) is reflected, for example, in a
massive increase in turnover on all the major securities markets and
in the explosion of the value of payments over the last decade.
Indeed, according to Bank for International Settlement (BIS) 1992
estimates, the ratio of annual value of financial transactions (measured as payments through the main interbank fund transfers
system) to GNP in the three countries with the largest financial
markets in the world grew dramatically and systematically, from
less than 10 per cent in 1970 to over 75 per cent in 1990 for the
United States, from just over 10 per cent in 1970 to over 110 per
cent in Japan, and from around 10 per cent in 1970 to over 40 per
cent in the United Kingdom!

Third, there has been an important trend for dissolution of
functional boundaries (where they existed, for example, in the

Table 3.5
Indicators of Growth in the Financial Industry

| Countries | *Share in value added to GNP or GDP(*)* | | |
	1970	*1979*	*1989*
United States	4.1	4.5	5.7+
Japan	4.5	4.9	5.6
United Kingdom(**)	12.5	14.8	20.0
Switzerland	4.6	5.8	10.1++
Germany	3.1	4.2	5.0
France	3.3	3.5	4.7
Spain	3.5	5.7	6.5
Australia(**)	8.5	9.0	12.1

(*) Plus imputed bank service charges, at current prices (1980 prices for
    France).
(**) Including real estate and business services.
(+) 1987   (++) 1985
Source: BIS, *62nd Annual Report* (Basle, BIS, 1992) p. 197

United Kingdom), particularly between banking and securities activities. This has led to the creation of increasingly complex institutions which integrate both types of activities.[6]

In those countries (like the United States and Japan) where barriers remain, banks are, however, free to combine banking and securities abroad, and are increasingly finding ways around the law in their home markets. Banks had been weakened during the last decade by a decline of underlying profitability partially – on the asset side – because they have lost some of their most profitable and safest business, as securitization reduced the demand for bank loans from prime borrowers, as commercial paper, corporate bonds and other types of direct financing displaced bank lending. It is also due – on the liabilities side – to the fact that banks have lost part of their core interest-free retail deposits, and are forced to bid for funds against each other, which has implied an increasing use of more expensive and less stable wholesale markets and a decline in the proportion of interest-free deposits. More broadly, as the cost of processing information fell, borrowers and lenders found it more feasible to deal with each other directly, and by-pass the banks. Partly to compensate for this decline in banks' profitability, banks, bank regulators and governments have started to break down remaining barriers between banking and securities markets, greatly enlarging banks' involvement in the securities business. This integration of banking and securities generates economics of scope and therefore benefits to the consumer, due both to lower costs based on joint 'production and marketing' and to greater convenience of purchasing different financial services from a single firm. However, it seems likely that it will increase the risks to the financial system as a whole. This is not because securities activities are inherently riskier than banking, but because securities activities are less regulated than banking activities and thus provide opportunities for additional risk-taking by aggressively managed banking institutions.[7] The integration of banking and securities' firms (even in countries with separate firms) could lead to conditions in which a shock coming from the securities market could spread through the banks and return (amplified) to the securities markets. The internationalization of both markets could make such a potential crisis international. Furthermore, because the pace of product innovation in securities markets is so rapid, risks in this area are increasingly difficult to assess, both by market actors and by regulators.

Though deregulation was broadly more limited in insurance, by the early 1990s a few countries (especially in Europe) had eased restrictions on the combination of insurance with banking business.

These changes have favored the creation of complex conglomerate structures, often across national borders, which combine traditional banking services with various types of securities and, more recently, with the provision of insurance. In the case of 'simple' banks, a greater proportion of their credit and liquidity exposures was incurred off the balance sheet.

Fourth, as hinted at above, there has been a vast expansion of available financial instruments, which was facilitated by the explosion of information technology. Many of these instruments (for example, futures, options, swaps) are very sophisticated, and the exact level of risk they generate is as yet unclear. As the range of financial instruments grew, a higher proportion became marketable. In the United States, even bank loans and company receivables have become marketable.

Finally, there was a greater institutionalization of savings, which provided a base for the expansion and greater sophistication of the securities markets. Their push towards international diversification was an important factor behind the internationalization and integration of markets.

Evaluation of Structural Changes in Financial Markets

Deregulation was driven by the perception that constraints on financial activity were ineffective or caused important inefficiencies in the allocation of capital and the operation of monetary policy. Deregulation acquired its own momentum as the elimination of restrictions in some areas led to pressure for their relaxation elsewhere. A third reason for deregulation grew from differences in regulatory treatment.

Deregulation has delivered important benefits.[8] Thus, both original suppliers and final users of funds are able to obtain better terms, via a richer and higher-yield range of financial assets and easier as well as cheaper access to external finance. Securitization is viewed not only to allow for lower costs, but also for longer maturities, which is crucial for the market viability of certain types of activities, that only become profitable in the long term. The abolition of foreign exchange controls and the broader process of globalization widened the international choice, both in terms of diversification of portfolios and sources of finance. At one level, the wider range of available financial instruments allows for better distribution and management of risk. Furthermore, the fall in transaction costs has increased the liquidity of securities markets. Finally, capital can flow more freely towards higher returns.

With regard to developing countries, the potential benefits of deregulation and globalization are particularly high, as capital is relatively scarce. Thus, the prospect of *larger inflows* via, for example, securities (particularly at a time when bank credit flows are far less likely to come in than in the past) and lower costs are especially attractive. It seems that certain instruments have been particularly beneficial in lowering the equity cost of capital in developing countries. Thus, international stock trading, through ADRs, for instance, has proved to be a valuable mechanism for lowering LDC companies' cost of capital decline. Furthermore, the issuing of ADRs is reported to lower costs not only for individual firms but also for other domestic firms via important spillover effects.[9]

The issues that need to be addressed are the costs which deregulation has brought about, and the measures that need to be taken (both nationally and internationally) to minimize those costs. Indeed, the changes brought about by deregulation and the freeing of market forces in the financial sector are creating new regulatory needs (such as capital adequacy requirements on financial institutions), which probably would not have existed had markets not been deregulated. It is argued in this chapter that these new regulatory challenges have only partly been met, and that urgent tasks (nationally, regionally and internationally) still need to be accomplished. This is largely because the development of market regulation tends to lag behind the changes that deregulation brought in the structure of the financial system. Particularly if the benefits of deregulation are valued, it is important to take measures that minimize costs, especially those that could disrupt, in a major way, the proper functioning of those markets, and have significant negative macroeconomic effects.

The costs of financial innovation relate to greater financial instability and fragility, reflected in the form of very large fluctuations in asset prices and/or distress among financial institutions. Both asset prices and exchange rates have gone through periods of sharp fluctuations in the last decade. As the BIS correctly points out, the main source of concern is not short-term volatility (which, if not extreme, is relatively harmless), but longer-term volatility especially when prices seem misaligned from their apparent sustainable levels, which leads both to misallocation of resources and the risk of large and disorderly changes.[10]

One particular aspect of the recent changes which may help

to explain capital market volatility is institutionalization of savings.[11] Indeed, some US commentators blamed fund managers' portfolio strategies for causing volatility at the time of the 1987 crash. More generally, the rise of global asset allocation as a tool of fund management, and the development of markets such as stock index futures, stimulated and facilitated massive growth in short-term cross-border equity flows. Though the investors wish to reduce risk by such strategies, the focus of funds on a small number of leveraged instruments often destabilizes markets and leads to sharp swings in asset prices. There is also evidence that switches of resources by large fund managers affect exchange-rate developments.

More generally, the greater internationalization and integration of the financial industry meant that shocks are more easily transmitted across borders as well as from one market to another. This is particularly well illustrated by the global nature of the stock market crashes of 1987 and 1989.

Furthermore, regular performance checks against the market (as frequent as monthly in the United States but less in the United Kingdom) may induce 'herding' among funds to avoid performing worse than the median fund, again with destabilizing effects on asset prices.

The problems of rapid switches between markets are likely to be of importance in an international context as well as in national markets. There is evidence that this is likely to have greater impact on volatility the smaller the market (as is the case for developing countries) and the greater the role played by foreign investors in it.

This is a special source of concern for developing countries, since traditionally the capital markets of LDCs show far greater volatility than those of industrialized economies. As can be seen in Table 3.6, the standard deviation of monthly percentage changes in share prices on the emerging markets were significantly higher than those of the US, UK or Japanese stock markets. This was particularly true for Latin American markets.

A second main reflection of increased financial instability and fragility is the fact that in the 1970s, and especially the 1980s, there have been several episodes of financial distress among financial enterprises. These include:

- the dollar overvaluation of the mid-1980s;

- the global stock market crash of October 1987, and the mini-crash two years later;

Table 3.6
Standard Deviation of Share Price Indexes

Market	Standard deviation five years ending December 1989	Standard deviation five years ending December 1992
Latin America		
Argentina	37.05	34.10
Brazil	21.07	23.06
Chile	8.26	7.56
Colombia	6.10	10.52
Mexico	16.09	10.52
Venezuela	11.59	14.37
East Asia		
Korea	8.16	9.00
Philippines	11.15	9.26
Taiwan, China	15.14	15.09
International Finance Corporation (IFC)		
Regional Indexes		
Composite	7.06	6.65
Latin America	13.91	9.11
Asia	7.98	7.94
Developed Markets		
United States (S&P 500)	5.16	3.79
United Kingdom (FT-100)	5.88	5.72
Japan (Nikkei)	4.08	8.64

Source: International Finance Corporation, *Emerging Stock Markets Factbook 1990* (Washington, DC: IFC, 1990) p. 58; and International Finance Corporation, *Emerging Stock Markets Factbook 1993* (Washington, DC: IFC, 1993) p. 50.

- property market crises (Japan, United Kingdom);

- extended banking crises (the secondary banking crisis in the United Kingdom, the savings and loan disaster in the United States, the collapse of the Nordic banking system);

- bankruptcies of large individual banks (Continental Illinois), or financial conglomerates (Bank of Credit and Commerce International, Maxwell);

- crises in the inter-bank market by spillovers of individual failure (Drexel Burnham Lambert, Herstatt), and

- accidents in the payment systems (Bank of New York).

It is important to emphasize that increasing instability in asset prices and institutional financial distress are related, as financial intermediaries hold – or lend against – the value of assets. As discussed above, banks in many countries have increased their securities business; they have also increased their exposure to real estate. As a consequence, their earnings – and their financial strength – became more sensitive to price fluctuations of both shares and real estate. Both the losses in securities markets and, especially, the weakness of real-estate prices have been significant in the recent problems faced by many banks.

INCREASES AND CHANGES IN THE NATURE OF RISKS

As a result of the changes in the structure and workings of the financial system, the nature and transmission of systemic risk changed significantly, and possibly increased. Systemic risk is defined by the BIS as 'the risk that the collapse or insolvency of one market will be transmitted to another participant'. Systemic risk is a macroeconomic phenomenon linking together different sources of financial instability. It is the unintentional outcome of externalities between decisions and conducts of individual agents under uncertainty.

The first major source of these externalities that poses a potential for systemic risk is the payment and settlements system. This has always been the main channel for the propagation of systemic crises, triggered usually by the inability of one or more institutions to settle their obligations. However, the explosion of the volume of financial transactions flows over the last decade has changed dramatically the scale of risks involved. These are concentrated in the inter-bank wholesale transfer systems. Banks participating in these systems now incur extremely large intra-day liquidity and credit exposures, possibly larger than the exposures traditionally captured in their balance sheets and frequently less closely monitored by regulators. This increases the vulnerability of the system to a participant's default or to technical failure, heightening the risk of a domino effect. These risks have been illustrated by the international ramifications of Herstatt's bankruptcy, by the technical failure of the Bank of New York and the unwinding of Drexel.

Settlement arrangements can be an independent source of systemic risk, besides being the channel through which counterparty risk is channelled. (Counterparty risk is the risk that the counterparty to a financial contract will not meet the terms of the contract.) These independent sources are due to: (a) possible computer breakdowns, (b) the concentration of risk in a clearing house which is inadequate to sustain the risk in a crisis, or (c) a possible incompatibility between timetables and legal obligations in different markets which increases the strain as turnover rises at a time of market disturbance. Indeed, strains that begin as a liquidity problem could become a solvency one. As an OECD study[12] points out, organized settlement systems offer the opportunity to reduce or redistribute risks in a way providing better protection for market participants and for the system as a whole.

Several recent reports have made various recommendations to improve and accelerate settlement arrangements, for example within and between national securities markets. These goals may take a long time to reach, due to legal problems as well as technological and cost factors. It seems that the greatest contribution to the management of risk can potentially come from achievement of delivery versus payment, shortening of settlement periods and the construction of legally valid systems of netting.

A second major source of systemic risk is increased exposure of institutions to market risks (the risk of losses in on-and-off balance-sheet positions – stemming from movements in market prices, including interest rates, exchange rates and equity values). This has happened because of the rapid development of securities and derivative markets, as well as foreign exchange contracts. Large variations in the market price of assets (for example, shares) are a very important source and channel of transmission of potential shocks. As positions are increasingly taken across a large number of markets, problems in one part of the market can quickly be transmitted to others. As BIS (1992) points out, the stock market crash of 1987 clearly illustrated how very different operating arrangements in different markets for highly substitutable instruments can have destabilizing effects because they result in differing price reaction speeds and uncoordinated stoppages.

The underlying force is that the deflation of assets prices destroys financial wealth. Because banks hold a large and increasing part of tradeable assets in their portfolios (due to the liberalization of banks' permitted range of activities and the rapid development of financial markets), or because they lent heavily to asset holders, the quality of bank assets can decline rapidly in such a situation.

The integration of market segments (and particularly that of banks and securities) thus increases the transmission of disturbances in financial markets. So do developments in information technology. The main potential channel for such transmission of disturbances is now the seizing up of funds in the wholesale markets or unwillingness for counterparties to enter into transaction with institutions whose soundness is in doubt, and not – as in the past – a generalized withdrawal of deposits.

This shows that, somewhat paradoxically given increased marketability of assets, the provision of liquidity has become more important in the new financial environment. Indeed, in the situation of a slump in asset prices, a key risk is that the liquidity of some market makers can be threatened, which provides a channel to spread instability between underlying and derivative markets. Because of the key importance of liquidity, banks continue to be at the heart of financial activity, even though their share of financial intermediation has fallen in several countries. Indeed, the 1987 stock market crash highlighted the need to keep open credit lines to securities and derivative market operators precisely to avoid systemic instability.

Special concerns with banks' exposure to market risks have recently (April 1993) led the Basle Committee on Banking Supervision to produce a consultative proposal on the supervisory treatment of market risks.[13] This proposal suggests that specific capital charges are applied to open positions in debt and equity securities in banks' trading portfolios and in foreign exchange; these capital charges should constitute a minimum prudential standard relative to the potential for losses that might occur for a given portfolio. These would complement the capital adequacy rules approved already by the BIS referring to banks' credit risks, which began to be implemented on January 1, 1993. Secondly, the proposed capital charges for each type of instrument would be roughly equivalent, in economic terms, to avoid creating artificial incentives favoring some instruments.

However, as will be discussed in the next section, regulation of banks' market risk (once implemented), though a positive development, will create problems of asymmetry with the regulation of securities' market risk, as coordination between banks' and securities' regulators (and among securities' regulators of different countries) has not yet been agreed.

Indeed, as it will be developed more in the next section, it would seem that large variations between different national regulations of financial firms (and especially securities) as well as fundamentally different approaches to regulation among banking and securities' regulators may themselves be, at least for a time, a third source of potential increase in systemic risk. Indeed, the OECD (1991) document implicitly recognizes this when it argues that:

> This diversity in regulatory coverage causes international systemic concern because it encourages regulatory arbitrage, leaves some significant risk-taking activities by intermediaries outside the supervisory net, fails to deliver a comprehensive supervisory oversight of conglomerates, and complicates the task of international co-operation among supervisory authorities.[14]

All this is a particularly important source for concern, because as the Federal Reserve Bank of New York put it in its 1985 Annual Report:

> A shock that starts in one market may spread quickly along this network of linkages until it finds a weakness in some seemingly unrelated place. In fact there is a growing tendency to build financial links along regulatory 'faultlines', where the responsibility for supervisory oversight is weak, divided, or cloudy.[15]

The issue of possible systemic risks arising from differences among supervisors, as well as supervisory gaps in certain markets and countries, is made more serious because financial markets have become more opaque, both for supervisors and market actors, in spite of all efforts. This opaqueness relates to instruments and relationships across instruments and markets as well as the organizational structure of institutions. Indeed, the growing complexity of organizational structures, for example international financial conglomerates, clouds the evaluation of the soundness of an institution. As the UK Bingham Report shows, the trend towards opaque corporate structures – and the problems it poses to regulators – are well illustrated by the Bank of Credit and Commerce International case.

One important question to ask is the extent to which the systemic risks associated with globalization and securitization are the same or different for flows going to developing countries. This question was insufficiently addressed in the existing literature and by policymakers. It can be tackled at three different levels:

- the level of investor protection,

- the level of global effects of possibly additional risks from flows to developing countries and

- the level referring to the additional sources of potential macroeconomic instability generated for developing countries by new types of flows.

The focus is on the third level, as the level which is of particular interest to LDCs. The first two levels seem far less a source of concern, given that the share of institutions' total investments going to developing countries is at present very low. Furthermore, with regards to global effects of a potential instability in LDCs, these effects are not considerably different from other global effects of financial instability previously discussed. However, this latter matter may require further study.

Regarding the potential additional sources of macroeconomic instability generated for LDCs by the new type of flows, the main one relates to balance-of-payments funding risk. To the extent that securities flows (and in particular international investment in equities) are potentially far more liquid than bank lending, foreign equity investors can move out very quickly in case of a balance of payments crisis or major devaluation. This would occur to the extent that – as is the case in many LDCs, and particularly in those LDCs experiencing large portfolio flows at present – there are no or very scarce relevant foreign exchange controls (see Table 3.7), and to the extent that the foreign equity investors would sell their shares to nationals of the LDC, and not to other foreigners.

Table 3.7
Entering and Existing Emerging Markets
A Summary of Investment Regulations (as of March 31, 1992)

Access *Are listed stocks* *freely available to* *foreign investors?*	*Repatriation of:* *Income* *(Dividends, interest,* *and realized capital)*	*Capital* *(Initial capital* *invested)*

Free Entry (No significant restrictions to purchasing stocks)

Argentina	free	free
Brazil	free	free
Colombia	free	free
Jordan	free	free
Malaysia	free	free
Pakistan	free	free
Peru	free	free
Portugal	free	free
Turkey	free	free

Relatively Free Entry (Some registration procedures required
to ensure repatriation rights)

Bangladesh	some restrictions	some restrictions
Chile	free	after 1 year
Costa Rica	some restrictions	some restrictions
Greece	some restrictions	some restrictions
Indonesia	some restrictions	some restrictions
Jamaica	some restrictions	some restrictions
Kenya	some restrictions	some restrictions
Mexico	free	free
Sri Lanka	some restrictions	some restrictions
Thailand	free	free
Trinidad & Tobago	relative free	relative free
Venezuela	some restrictions	some restrictions

continued on next page

Table 3.7 continued

Access Are listed stocks freely available to foreign investors?	Repatriation of: Income (Dividends, interest, and realized capital)	Capital (Initial capital invested)

Special Classes of Shares (Foreigners restricted to certain classes of stock, designated for foreign investors)

China	some restrictions	some restrictions
Korea	free	free
Philippines	free	free
Zimbabwe	restricted	restricted

Authorized Investors Only (Only approved foreign investors may buy stocks)

India	some restrictions	some restrictions
Taiwan, China	free	free

Closed (Closed or access severely restricted, for example, for non-resident nationals only)

Nigeria	some restrictions	some restrictions

Note: In some countries, industries which are considered strategic are not available to foreign/non-resident investors and the level of foreign investment in other cases may be limited by national law or corporate policy to minority positions not to aggregate more than 49 per cent of voting stock. The summaries above refer to 'new money' investment by foreign institutions; other regulations may apply to capital invested through debt-conversion schemes or other sources.

Key to Repatriation: Some restrictions – Typically, requires some registration with or permission of Central Bank, Ministry of Finance, or an office of exchange controls that may restrict the timing of exchange release. Free – Repatriation done routinely.

Source: International Finance Corporation, *Emerging Stock Markets Factbook 1992* (Washington, DC: IFC, 1992) p. 74.

Naturally, new foreign investment in such equities would also cease at that time. The result would be additional pressure on the balance of payments and on the exchange rate, possibly contributing either to a major balance-of-payments crisis and/or to a large devaluation. Both would have undesirable effects on the LDC economy's levels of output and of inflation. Therefore, in a pre-balance of payments or exchange-rate crisis situation, large international equity outflows (in relation to the domestic economy) could seriously magnify problems arising from other sources.

This is not just related to international equity flows, nor is it a purely LDC problem, as is clearly illustrated by the effect of private financial flows in September 1992 on several currencies in the European Monetary System (EMS). Indeed, there have been reports that some investors who were involved in the 'speculative' flows that so seriously affected some of the then EMS currencies, are now 'going into Latin America'.[16] However, the scale of the impact could be larger for LDCs, given the smaller size of their economies and *their greater fragility*, and the special features of their securities markets.

Furthermore, as discussed above, price volatility of LDC stock markets is in general higher than that for developed countries. Therefore, the impact of potentially large sales by foreign investors (or nationals with a 'transnational' mentality) would be to depress significantly the prices of shares. This could, via a wealth effect, contribute to a decline in aggregate demand and/or lead to other forms of financial instability. This latter would especially be the case to the extent that in the particular LDC there was strong integration of banking and securities, development of financial conglomerates, etc.

Other special features of LDC stock exchanges also increase their potential for generating negative effects in other parts of the economy. These relate, for example, in some countries to inaccurate and slow settlements procedures. As discussed above, this increases instability in the stock exchanges that can spill over to other sectors. Furthermore, the LDC stock markets tend to suffer from a shortage of good-quality, large capitalization shares. This can result in quick overheating (that is, rapid increases in prices) when domestic and international interest is generated in these markets, due to some positive shock of expectations, and in quick 'overcooling' (that is, rapid falls in prices), due to some negative shock of expectations, as discussed above.

Though on the whole foreign direct investment flows are far

more stable and long term, it has been reported that international companies often do play the 'lead and lag game' with some of their funds, for example in anticipation of a devaluation, and that this 'speculative' behavior can be an additional, though probably a more limited, source of exchange-rate instability.[17]

With regard to bonds held by foreign investors, two problems could arise. First, if investors saw the risk of a crunch coming, there could be fears that the seniority of bonds (which has been an important factor in attracting bond finance to LDCs) could be reversed; this fear will be increased to the extent that bonds become a high proportion of the LDCs' debt. Second, as the bonds and their interest are denominated in foreign exchange, if there are fears of a large devaluation, then foreign investors would fear an increase in their credit risk. For both reasons, investors in bonds might want to sell if a balance-of-payments or exchange-rate crisis was foreseen. To the extent that these bonds could be sold to nationals of the LDC (which seems more difficult than in the case of shares), then this would have a balance-of-payment and/or exchange-rate effect.

Last, but certainly not least, regarding inflows to LDCs, and especially to Latin America, there is a fairly high proportion of these inflows that come in for a very short period (for example, 3 months) mainly attracted by interest-rate differentials. Naturally, these flows are highly volatile, and in the case of a threat of a balance-of-payments or exchange-rate crisis, would leave very rapidly and with destabilizing effects.

Finally, it should be stressed that such major and rapid outflows of capital from an LDC are far more likely to occur if there is a large macroeconomic imbalance in that economy. Therefore, in the current world of globalization and free capital flows, the importance of prudent macroeconomic policies is paramount. With prudent macro-management, large, sudden outflows that are particularly destabilizing are far less likely, though they cannot be completely ruled out. Indeed, the recent Group of Ten (G–10) Dini Report acknowledges that even for the case of developed countries, 'a country can ... experience downward pressure on its currency despite the fact that its macroeconomic policy and performance have been sound'.[18]

EXISTING SUPERVISION AND REGULATION – SOME LIMITATIONS

The changing nature and possible increase of systemic risk implies a number of major challenges and issues for governments. The first one is to improve prudential regulation and supervision of individual institutions, so as to curb excessive risk-taking at the source.

One issue that needs clarifying is that of *coverage* of regulation and supervision; this should cover all those financial companies whose collapse would trigger systemic turmoil. Though there is considerable consensus[19] that supervisory coverage limited to banks may well not be enough, a number of major supervisory gaps still exist. Probably the most obvious is one that allows some securities houses to carry out certain activities via unsupervised affiliates. Above all, there are important differences in the extent and form in which similar institutions are regulated in different jurisdictions. Furthermore, there are important differences in how varying institutions are regulated both in the same and in different jurisdictions (see below).

An important issue in this context is whether institutions should be supervised on a consolidated basis. The questions are (a) if legal and economic separation of, for example, banking and securities can be achieved (which is in itself very complex), and (b) if 'firewalls' established to limit transfer of capital between them will be sufficient to separate the market perception of the credit standing of both institutions, and therefore isolate one unit from the other in a period of distress. As the Drexel case illustrated, funding seems to be withdrawn from institutions that are sound, due to associations in the public mind with problems arising in affiliates. Therefore, failure to consolidate can result in serious supervisory gaps. Though consolidation is a standard practice in banking supervision (following in particular the problems caused by Banco Ambrosiano), it is not yet generally accepted in the supervision of securities and insurance.

Consolidation of supervision between different types of activities is made difficult by conceptual differences among their regulators, based on key differences in the nature of their business. The most fundamental difference between securities and banks is that the former have a far shorter commercial time horizon than banks. Banks typically hold loans on their balance sheets until maturity, while securities firms experience rapid asset turnover.

Because the bulk of securities firm assets are marketable, they are therefore subject to severe pressures in periods of market downturn (which leads therefore to market risk), and to a similar decline in the firm's net worth. Because firms need to meet losses quickly, securities regulators emphasize liquidity, treating illiquid assets consecutively and often allowing certain forms of short-term subordinated financing to be counted as capital. Since the key concern is that securities firms should be able to run themselves down in a very short period *and* meet their liabilities so that their clients/counterparties will not incur losses, the key supervisory test is that of net liquid assets. Thus, a firm should have liquid assets (valued at current price) which – after allowance for possible reductions in the value of the assets before they could be sold – exceed total liabilities. In contrast, a major proportion of bank assets are traditionally non-marketable; as a result, the main risk for banks is credit risk.

Differing from securities houses, banks are not expected to respond to financial problems by going out of business, since their assets could only be sold at a heavy discount, implying losses for creditors and depositors. Therefore, the main objective of bank regulators is to sustain banks as going concerns, especially because bank failures involve risks to the financial system as a whole. Consequently, bank supervisors tend to focus far less on liquidity and short-run changes in asset values, and more on the long-run viability of the bank. Therefore, the regulatory definition of capital only included financing instruments of a more permanent nature (excluding, for example, subordinated debt from primary capital).

Regulatory differences extend also to the role of deposit insurance and lender of last resort, which are important for banks, but are on the whole unavailable for securities.

The above differences in the regulation of banks and securities firms have led to difficulties for policymakers of the European Community (EC) in their attempts to establish an appropriate regulatory framework for a single European financial market. The EC Directive on the Capital Adequacy of Investment Firms and Credit Institutions (known as CAD) allows alternative definitions of capital for the supervisors of non-bank investment firms and for banks undertaking securities activities. As Dale points out, 'These alternative definitions of capital are, of course, intended to meet the policy objective of ensuring a level playing field between banks and non-bank investment firms.'[20] However, there is a concern that these capital rules are *not* justified on prudential grounds.

In particular, though the appropriate regulatory goal defined by the European Community for bank supervisors is solvency, the EC regulatory objective for securities is more limited, to protect investors and counterparties without necessarily ensuring solvency. This is a goal that can be achieved by more liberal use of subordinated debt. But, as discussed above, given the way that securities markets developed and the Drexel episode led to a crisis of confidence in the investment firms, the EC objectives seem inappropriate or at least insufficient to deal with systemic risk.

Thus, the main problem with the EC capital adequacy directive seems to be its focus on establishing a level playing field between banks and non-bank investment firms, while failing to address the more fundamental policy dilemma, namely that increasingly in non-banking financial markets similar systemic risks can be created as occurred previously only in narrower banking systems. If the official safety net were extended by national authorities to activities like securities, then the problem of subsidized – and thus excessive – risk-taking could be extended from banks to securities.

Indeed, the EC approach seems to accentuate these problems, as it allows banks to dilute their capital, while allowing the risk of cross-infection from securities activities to increase. Besides the problems of new regulations in the European Community (EC), there is the issue that the EC and the United States seem to be moving in opposite directions in the key issue of risk segregation. Thus, in the EC it is increasingly assumed that a bank would always stand behind a related securities firm; in the United States, the new holding company and firewall structure is designed explicitly so that a securities firm in trouble is *not* supported by its bank affiliate. This may imply that in Europe the lender-of-last-resort function could be extended (directly or indirectly) to bank-related securities firms. In contrast, the US arrangement (which assumes that firewalls, and other mechanisms, can separate effectively risks between banking and their securities branches) would restrict the official safety net only to banking.

The coexistence of these sharply opposed structures could be particularly problematic in times of global financial stress. Thus, in the EC, the temptation could arise for lenders to move their exposure from independent to bank-related securities, as the latter are more likely to get official support. Furthermore, in those circumstances, there would be a strong incentive for lenders to withdraw their exposure from US securities in favor of securities firms that are affiliates of European banks. Such large moves could accentuate financial distress in the United States, and globally.

Indeed, differences in the perception of securities regulators (and particularly between those of the United States and of the rest of the countries) have impeded a global agreement on capital requirements of securities firms (which would have done for securities what the Basle accord has done for banking). An attempt to reach such an agreement was made, after much preparatory work, at the International Organization of Securities Commissions (IOSCO) Annual Conference in 1992; unfortunately, this attempt failed.[21] It should, however, be mentioned that IOSCO did reach some important agreements, such as the approval of principles for regulation of financial conglomerates.[22]

Perhaps equally serious is the fact that had IOSCO been able to agree on common risk measures and capital adequacy rules for securities, this would have served as a basis for a joint framework (to be elaborated by the BIS and IOSCO) for commercial banks, investment banks and securities houses. As a result of this inability to reach agreement within IOSCO, the Basle Committee has launched its own suggestions (discussed above) to limit market and other related risks for securities activities carried out by banks, by setting capital requirements on them. If approved, this will cover an important supervisory gap, but will still leave a very large gap in the regulation of non-bank securities.

As a result, supervision and regulation globally is patchy and very uneven. Indeed, as can be clearly seen in Table 3.8, while securities firms and financial conglomerates outside the European Community will *not* in the next few years have to adhere to any international guidelines, banks inside the EC will have to meet three different sets of rules for measuring market risks and for capital requirements to cover those risks, the BIS ones, the EC directives and possibly some national ones. The issue is made more complex by the fact that Basle rules are stricter than the EC's directive, for example, with regards to capital requirements on foreign exchange risk.

As can be seen in Table 3.8, banks are regulated by up to three sets of regulators in an EC country like the United Kingdom. They are regulated internationally by the 1988 Basle Accord and will probably be regulated by Basle on their securities activities; banks are also regulated in a country like the United Kingdom by its own national regulations and by the EC capital adequacy directive. On the other hand, neither securities

Table 3.8
Regulatory Frameworks of Financial Institutions

	Inter-national	*EC*[3]	*USA*	*UK*
Banks	x[1]	xx	x	xxx
Securities	–	x	x	xx
Financial Conglomerates	–[2]	x	x[4]	x

(1) Includes both the 1988 Accord and the regulation of securities activities of banks, the latter proposed in 1993 and to be implemented by 1997 at the earliest.
(2) There is an IOSCO proposal for principles on which to regulate financial conglomerates, but no formal regulatory agreement.
(3) EC directives to be enacted by 1996.
(4) Until recently, US regulation of non-bank securities houses, within major financial groups, was practically non-existent.

Source: Table prepared by the author, on the basis of interview material, BIS and IOSCO documents, and Richard Dale, *International Banking Deregulation: The Great Banking Experiment* (Oxford, England: Blackwell, 1992).

nor financial conglomerates outside the European Community have any form of international regulation, though there are national regulations for securities; for the EC countries, there are special EC regulations approved or in the process of approval for securities and financial conglomerates.

It would seem that, unless special efforts are made to overcome this asymmetry, it is likely to remain for quite a number of years. This relates not only to the conceptual differences between regulators discussed above (which originate largely in the diversity between different financial institutions and their differences among individual countries), but also due to institutional differences, for example between BIS and IOSCO. The BIS carries a lot of weight, as it provides the basis for a 'central bank of central banks'. Its members, the G–10 central banks, also are the lenders of last resort of their own banking systems. Its work on international harmonization of supervisory standards has gone on for around 20 years. Therefore it seems to find it easier to reach agreements than IOSCO, which is a far newer institution; though created in 1974 mainly by Latin American institutions, it became international only in 1987. Its work on harmonization of international regulations is thus far more recent than that of the BIS. It represents bodies from 51 countries, which in itself makes it more difficult to reach agreement than in a G–10 institution. Furthermore, the bodies whose activities it coordinates (the securities commissions) themselves tend to be fairly young, and do not have special lender-of-last-resort powers domestically. For these reasons it may also well continue to be more difficult to reach agreements on common regulations, and to enforce those agreements, in securities than it is in banking-related activities. EC directives, once formally approved (which tend to imply a long process), do have enforceable sanctions as they follow a legal process (unlike both the BIS and IOSCO).

Though all this is understandable, it does pose serious additional risks to the financial system originated in regulations' asymmetries. Problems can take place even in cases where regulations are integrated, for example because contract law exists at a national level and therefore cannot be integrated. This is particularly an issue in so far as there is growth of transactions whose settlement is at a future date.

The differences of laws among countries can affect, for example, liquidation proceedings of collapsed financial institutions, to favor one group of national creditors against the rest.[23] It therefore not only creates inequalities internationally, but also imposes additional pressures on settling situations of financial failure. The promotion of international treaties, for example, via the United Nations, the General Agreement on Tariffs and Trade (GATT) or other bodies, though complex to achieve, would need to play an important role to help overcome these types of problems internationally, whereas in the context of the European Community these problems would decrease as integration progresses.

Besides the general issues relating to supervision and regulation in the new financial environment, it seems important to emphasize that there may be specific issues posed by the new types of risk generated by the impact of these new trends specifically related to LDCs. Though national securities regulators do have special treatment for firms investing in LDCs (which, for example, in the case of the United Kingdom discriminates some-what between different types of LDCs, mainly related to the quality of regulations of the countries' stock exchange),[24] the focus on LDCs seems somewhat limited, for example, not taking into account macroeconomic developments in those countries even in the context of its possible impact on investor protection.

On the broader issue of the effects of financial flows on macroeconomic performance of countries (and specifically LDCs), this is explicitly *not* a matter of concern to any of the regulatory bodies, unless it affects the potential solvency of the financial institutions which they regulate.[25] This poses the need for other international institutions, like the International Monetary Fund (IMF), possibly for regional bodies, and/or last but certainly not least for the national recipient governments to closely monitor the impact of such flows on current and future macroeconomic trends in the LDCs, and possibly to define specific regulations to influence the level and composition of such flows.

CONCLUSIONS AND POLICY RECOMMENDATIONS

There is a growing consensus that global financial deregulation and liberalization, though having many positive effects, have also resulted both in greater risks for the global financial system and for individual investors. As Richard Breuer, Member of the Board of Managing Directors of the Deutsche Bank, succinctly put it: 'This leads to a need for re-regulation and harmonization of supervisory legislation.'[26] This does not mean a return to the types of regulations that existed in the 1970s, but to regulations appropriate for the needs of the new financial system of the 1990s, resulting largely from deregulation.

Though it may seem somewhat paradoxical, the more free-enterprise-oriented a country is, the greater the role of official supervision of financial institutions will be. This is due to the fact that in a truly market-oriented economy, the danger of business failures will be high, leading to greater risk to the balance sheets of the financial institutions lending to the business sector. Especially if governments and central banks wish *not* to bail out financial institutions, then deregulation needs to be supported by close and well-coordinated supervision of financial institutions.

From the above analysis, it can be seen that to achieve close and coordinated supervision of financial institutions globally a number of important tasks need to be accomplished. These pose an important and difficult challenge to governments and especially to regulators.

First, the issue of appropriate and coordinated supervision of securities needs to be dealt with far quicker than in recent years. Though the recent Basle consultative proposal makes a valuable effort in dealing with the complex issues of regulating capital adequacy for banks' securities activities, no equivalent basis exists yet for non-banks' securities. This is an important regulatory gap that needs to be filled fairly urgently. As discussed briefly above, this will need, as a precondition, to overcome the differences in regulatory approach to risks in securities, between the United States and other countries, and in particular the European Community. Furthermore, to achieve a more closely integrated system of supervision of internationally active intermediaries in securities markets, this would probably require securities regulators to develop their equivalent of the Basle Concordat for banking supervisors, defining the responsibilities of a lead regulator in the home country in relation to host countries.

Second, more generally, a serious effort needs to be made to extend regulatory coverage to financial institutions that are now effectively unregulated, such as financial conglomerates. This requires closer coordination between banking and securities supervisors. If this is not done, competitive realities will continue to lead to a shift of business away from more regulated to less regulated entities, increasing the risks to the safety and soundness of the financial system.

Third, though agreements on capital requirements for banks – and hopefully in the near future for their securitized activities – in the context of Basle provide a key regulatory input, there also needs to be a large effort to reach agreements on standards such as for accounting and disclosure. These agreements need to be reached first globally within each financial industry's regulators (for example, banking, securities and insurance) and then agreements to coordinate such standards need to be arranged. Particular emphasis needs to be placed on integrating LDC representatives into these efforts, since their standards may often be lower or particularly different from those of the developed countries.

Fourth, additional work needs to be done to improve specific aspects, such as, the organization of settlements systems for securities, so as to prevent them from acting as an independent source of systemic risk. Organized settlement systems offer the opportunity to reduce or redistribute risks in a way that provides better protection both for participants in markets and for the system as a whole. Among the measures necessary to improve and accelerate settlement arrangements within and between national securities markets are: shorter settlement periods, links between settlement arrangements in home and host countries and, especially, the achievement of simultaneous good delivery of securities against payment for them.

Fifth, as discussed above, there may be an increasing need to achieve greater global integration of contract law, so that contracts can be challenged internationally, and regulators can carry out liquidation proceedings that are internationally equitable. Such legal integration would both facilitate further global financial integration and aid the task of regulators in effectively and equitably enforcing their regulations. Naturally this task poses difficult issues relating to the promotion of international treaties.

Sixth, the issues raised above – and others raised by globalization and increased complexity of finance – seem to require creation of a strong and ongoing institutional capacity at the international level. At a minimum, this would require in particular a substantial strengthening of IOSCO and a closer integration of all countries into the Basle Accord. A more ambitious approach – both far more difficult to implement and far more satisfactory – would be to create a global board of regulators,[27] with central banks and other regulatory representatives, and possibly with members drawn from the private sector. Such a body could set mutually acceptable minimum capital requirements for all major financial institutions, establish uniform trading, reporting and disclosure standards and monitor the performance of markets and financial institutions.

One of the virtues of such an approach is that it would increasingly achieve a truly global perspective on regulation, integrating both different national and functional perspectives. At present, such global perspectives are difficult to achieve since regulators respond to their constituencies and their conceptual frameworks (both at a national level and at a functional level). This is clearly a more long-term task.

Besides the above described initiatives at a regulatory level, two initiatives can be suggested, one that specifically focuses on LDCs and the second on a proposal for an international tax. There is an urgent specific need to monitor precisely the scale and composition of capital inflows into developing countries. Due to the rapid pace of innovation, and to other factors, this is no easy task. Important efforts are being carried out in this area by the World Bank and the IMF. Beyond monitoring, it is necessary to assess the present and likely future macroeconomic impact of such flows on the LDCs. There may be fears that the scale and/or composition of the flows is having important undesirable effects, for example on overvaluing exchange rates via a 'financial Dutch disease phenomenon' (see Glossary) which will discourage export growth; or there may be related fears that a dramatic reverse of large flows could have negative future effects, on output or inflation, as occurred in the debt crises of the 1980s (though the mechanisms would be slightly different). In such situations, there may be a case for measures to be taken to discourage excessive inflows, especially of certain types of flows (for example, shorter-term ones).

An important issue is – institutionally – who should take the initiative? Clearly the first level is that of national LDC governments; thus, the Chilean, Mexican and Brazilian governments have taken measures in recent years. Second, regional institutions, for example, the UN Economic Commission on Latin America and the Caribbean, and/or regional development banks, for example, the Inter-American Development Bank (IDB) can take an interest.

Third, global institutions, particularly the IMF and the World Bank need to take an interest, and exert influence, especially to the extent that insufficient action takes place at the national level. The dispute between the Argentine government and the IMF on the need for reserve requirements on capital inflows provides a good example.

Above all, such actions need to be guided by the principle that the capital inflows to LDCs should contribute to long-term growth and development, and that future debt or major foreign exchange crises need to be avoided. The last LDC debt crisis displayed the 'sins of omission' by different key actors. It also exposed relevant lessons for the management of the new type of private flows of the 1990s, so that their long-term effect is more beneficial and sustained.

Finally, a measure that may deserve attention is Tobin's proposal to levy an international uniform tax on spot transactions in foreign exchange.[28] The aim would be to slow down speculative, short-term capital flows movements (which would be more affected since by definition they cross borders often, and would be taxed every time), while having only a marginal effect on long-term flows. This would somewhat increase the autonomy of national authorities for monetary and macroeconomic policy, with a bit more independence from the effects of international money markets. Such an autonomy would be particularly valuable for LDCs, to the extent that their economies adapt less easily to external shocks and because their thinner financial markets are more vulnerable to the impact of external capital inflows and outflows. The proposal would be particularly attractive to LDCs if the proceeds of it were to go, as Tobin suggested, to the World Bank.

This proposal is different from the other seven listed above, in that it may seem more radical. However, there is a widespread feeling, even in private circles, that financial liberalization may have proceeded too far or at least too fast, and that financial liberalization carried to the extreme may even risk damaging the far more important trade liberalization, whose benefits are far more universally recognized. Furthermore, a new tax would be attractive to fiscally constrained governments.

Therefore, a small tax on financial flows – which particularly discourages short-term flows – could be a welcome development. It could be introduced on a temporary basis for a fixed period, for example, five years. This would be consistent with the fairly widespread perception that financial fragility and systemic risk are particularly high in the current stage, of 'transition' from regulated to deregulated financial markets.

The tax would have an additional advantage. It could greatly facilitate monitoring of international financial flows, by providing centralized data bases on such flows. This could be particularly valuable for innovative flows and flows going to LDCs where particular information gaps exist.

Doubtless technical problems would need to be overcome. An institution like the IMF would be very competent to deal with them. More seriously, probably, would be the opposition of certain parts of the financial community, which would lobby against such a proposal. However, the attractiveness of the idea, and an apparent increase in support for that type of initiative, could lead to such an innovative measure to be taken globally.

Notes

1. The authors thank Luis Gonzalez for very valuable research assistance. Dr Stephany Griffith-Jones is grateful to regulators who offered her valuable insights when she interviewed them. The responsibility, however, for her views and ideas as expressed in this chapter is hers.
2. See, for example, World Bank, *Global Economic Prospects and the Developing Countries* (Washington, DC: World Bank, 1993) pp. 35–6.

3. World Bank, *Global Economic Prospects and the Developing Countries*.
4. See World Bank, *Global Economic Prospects and the Developing Countries*; World Institute for Development Economics Research (WIDER), *Foreign Portfolio Investment in Emerging Equity Markets*, Study Group Series no. 5 (Helsinki, Finland: WIDER, 1990); Sudarshan Gooptu, 'Portfolio Investment Flows to Emerging Markets', *World Bank Working Paper*, WPS 1117 (Washington, DC: World Bank, March 1993).
5. World Bank, *Global Economic Prospects and the Developing Countries*.
6. For a detailed analysis of this trend, see Richard Dale, *International Banking Deregulation: The Great Banking Experiment* (Oxford, England: Blackwell, 1992).
7. Dale, *International Banking Deregulation: The Great Banking Experiment*, p. 44 and p. 193.
8. See, for example, Bank for International Settlement (BIS), *62nd Annual Report* (Basle: BIS, June 15, 1992); also Richard O'Brien, *Global Financial Integration: The End of Geography* (London: Pinter Publishers, 1992; published in North America for the Royal Institute of International Affairs: New York: Council on Foreign Relations Press, 1992).
9. World Bank, *Global Economic Prospects and the Developing Countries*.
10. Bank for International Settlement (BIS), *62nd Annual Report*.
11. See, for example, E. Philip Davis, 'The Structure, Regulation and Performance of Pension Funds in Nine Industrial Countries' (mimeo, Bank of England, 1992); also Michael Howell and Angela Cozzini, *Games without Frontiers: Global Equity Markets in the 1990s* (London: Salomon Brothers, 1991).
12. Organization for Economic Cooperation and Development (OECD), 'Systemic Risks in Securities Markets' in *Financial Market Trends*, vol. 49 (June 1991) pp. 13–18.
13. This proposal is part of the consultative proposal on 'The Prudential Supervision of Netting, Market Risks and Interest Rate Risk' and can be found in Stephany Griffith-Jones with Vassilis Papageorgiou, 'Globalisation of Financial Markets and Impact on Flows to LDCs: New Challenges for Regulation', Annex 1 in Jan Joost Teunissen (ed.), *The Pursuit of Reform: Global Finance and the Developing Countries* (The Hague, The Netherlands: Forum on Debt and Development (FONDAD), 1993) pp. 94–7.
14. OECD, 'Systemic Risks in Securities Markets', p. 16.
15. Edward J. Frydl, 'The Challenges of Financial Change' in Federal Reserve Bank of New York, *Annual Report 1985* (New York: Federal Reserve Bank of New York, April 1986) pp. 3–27.
16. Interview material.
17. Interview material.
18. Group of Ten (G–10), *International Capital Movements and Foreign Exchange Markets*, A Report to the Ministers and Governors by the Group of Deputies, (Rome: Group of Ten, 1993) p. 36.

19. See, for example, BIS, *62nd Annual Report.*
20. Dale, *International Banking Deregulation: The Great Banking Experiment,* p. 166.
21. Interview material; see also 'Capital Spat' in *The Economist,* October 31, 1992; and 'Tough Time Making a Level Playing Field' in *Financial Times,* May 4, 1993.
22. International Organization of Securities Commissions (IOSCO), *Final Communiqué of the 17th Annual Conference* (London: IOSCO, October 1992).
23. Interview material.
24. Interview material.
25. Interview material.
26. Richard Breuer, 'Financial Integration: The End of Geography', paper prepared for the International Organization of Securities Commissions (IOSCO), XVII Annual Conference, London, October 1992.
27. H. Kaufmann, at the IOSCO XVII Annual Conference, in London, October 1992, suggested the creation of such a body, and called it 'Board of Overseers of Major International Institutions and Markets'.
28. James Tobin, 'Tax the Speculators' in *Financial Times,* December 22, 1992.

4 Exchange Arrangements in Support of Development

Avadhoot R. Nadkarni

INTRODUCTION

The importance of exchange arrangements in the context of free trade and world development has been recognized by the world community at least since the Bretton Woods conference. The conference instituted the par-value system for the determination of exchange rates. The system was instituted for the explicit purposes of facilitating the expansion and balanced growth of international trade which contributes to the promotion and maintenance of high levels of employment and real incomes, as well as to the development of the productive resources of all members. These purposes were enshrined in Article I (ii) of the International Monetary Fund's (IMF) Articles of Agreement. Since Bretton Woods, a stable international financial environment has been regarded as necessary in a complex and interdependent world. The exchange-rate arrangements that emerged after the break-up of the Bretton Woods system have two main weaknesses:

- From an immediate perspective, some aspects of the arrangements (for example, the volatility and the misalignment of the exchange rates of major currencies) inflict real costs on participating countries, with the less developed countries (LDCs) carrying a relatively larger burden.

- From a longer-term perspective, the current *ad hoc* arrangements do not adequately promote an integrated world economy, which is a prerequisite for the rational and sustainable development of all countries' productive resources.

72

The exchange arrangements proposed here are based on the following premises:

- A relatively stable exchange-rate system will require and will eventually promote the policy coordination among countries necessary for institutions like a World Central Bank and a single world currency to evolve. Such world institutions are necessary in the long run for the governance of a complex and interdependent world.[1]

- The increasing integration of the developing countries into the market-based system of the developed world inflicts certain costs on the LDCs. Among the real costs to the LDCs are those accompanying the excessive devaluations required to maintain balance-of-payments sustainability during the process of opening up of their economies. To the extent that such an integration is in the interest of both the developing and the developed world, LDCs should be compensated for the costs incurred.

- Such compensation should be provided as a matter of right through resources generated in the very working of the international financial system, such as those from seigniorage benefits that would accrue in the creation of a single currency.

These three premises correspond to three important characteristics of any exchange arrangement: the flexibility versus fixity of exchange rates of national currencies; the valuation of the national currencies, that is, the levels at which the exchange rates of the currencies are determined, and the reserve standard of the system, that is, the asset used for settling payments imbalances and creating the unit of account among currencies. The three subsequent sections of this chapter will discuss an ideal exchange arrangement in terms of these three characteristics.

The first section of this chapter brings out the LDCs' preference for relatively stable exchange rates. It argues that the recent shift toward more flexible exchange-rate arrangements, including independent floating of currencies by LDCs, does not reflect a definite LDC preference for such flexible arrangements. It calls for the establishment of fixed nominal parities as a precondition for the policy coordination necessary for the ultimate establishment of a more efficient governance of the world economy. The second section describes some of the real costs of excessive devaluations of LDC currencies. It distinguishes between Cassel's concept of the purchasing power parity exchange rate and Nurkse's concept of the exchange rate required to maintain a balance-of-payments equilibrium. It also suggests that it is necessary for LDCs to have fixed exchange rates in order to ensure balance-of-payments sustainability and that exchange rates need to be fixed according to the Nurksian concept. It proposes that the difference between the two rates indicates the costs the LDCs sustain when they open up their economies. Hence, this difference can be used to determine the compensation that should be paid to the LDCs. The third section discusses the possibilities of how such a compensation can be paid in terms of an international asset.

THE STABILITY OF EXCHANGE RATES

Through their pronouncements and practice the developing countries have always preferred a relatively stable if not a fixed exchange-rate system at the global level. This preference is understandable, given the LDCs' costs of misaligned and volatile exchange rates since the major currencies have started to float.[2]

In 1972, following the initial collapse of the Bretton Woods system of exchange rates, the IMF established a Committee on Reform of the International Monetary System and Related Issues, more commonly known as the Committee of Twenty (C–20) which included nine LDC representatives. In its 'Outline of Reform', the C–20 clearly opted for an exchange-rate mechanism 'based on stable but adjustable par values'.[3] The final document was influenced by compromises, especially between France and the United States. Nevertheless, as a group, the LDCs had emphasized *stability* more than *adjustability*. Of course, the experience of the later Bretton Woods period had taught the importance of timely adjustment of parities. Over the years the futility of seeking a stable exchange-rate regime in the absence of improved macroeconomic policy coordination among major countries became apparent; LDCs' response, at least up to the late 1980s, was not to opt for greater flexibility of exchange rates, but for greater policy coordination among the major developed countries. This is evident from a review of several Communiqués issued by the Group of Twenty-Four (G–24).

In the absence of a global regime of fixed exchange rates, the LDCs continued to seek some anchor for their exchange rates on the rough seas of the generalized floating of major currencies. Thus the initial reaction of the LDCs to the generalized floating was to tie their currencies to one of the major currencies. As reported in the *International Financial Statistics*[4] table on exchange-rate arrangements, nearly 90 per cent of the LDC members of the IMF, that is, 86 out of the 97 LDC members, adopted single-currency pegs during the turbulent period of March–July 1973. Pegging to a single major currency (such as the US dollar) under a system of generalized floating of major currencies is, of course, not the same as a system of globally fixed exchange rates. The former implies floating against all other currencies which are not pegged to that same currency (the dollar). The stability imparted by pegging to a single currency is deceptive,[5] unless a major part of the trade and financial relations of the pegging country is with the country whose currency is adopted as a peg (the United States). Pegging to a single currency stabilizes *one* exchange rate but not the *average* of the exchange rates of the pegging currency *vis-a-vis* other currencies. That is, it does not stabilize what has come to be called 'the effective exchange rate'. Under a system of generalized floating, it is more important to stabilize the effective exchange rate. This would require pegging to a basket of currencies rather than to a single currency.[6]

Only three LDCs (Malta, Morocco and Cyprus) adopted the basket peg exchange-rate arrangement during the turbulent period of March–July 1973, immediately after the advent of generalized floating but before the popularization of the basket concept by the adoption of the SDR valuation basket in July 1974. The practice gained grounds over the years with 40 out of 130 LDC members of the IMF (about one-third) pegging to currency composites in 1987.[7] The widespread practice of basket-pegging reflected the LDCs' best effort to recreate, to the extent possible, the stability of the Bretton Woods system. Since all the exchange rates were fixed to each other in the Bretton Woods system, consequently the effective exchange rate of any currency was fixed as well. On the other hand, pegging a currency (for example, the rupee) to a basket of currencies (for example, the US dollar and the British pound) where the currencies in the basket are floating in relation to each other, stabilizes the effective exchange rate but not the individual exchange rates. This is the case because a change in the value of any currency in the basket (for example, the dollar) requires that all other exchange rates be adjusted. That is, in our example, the nominal exchange rate of rupee to pound needs to be changed as well.

LDCs and Floating Exchange Rates

It should be noted that only two LDC currencies, those of Lebanon and the Philippines, were floating independently in the turbulent period of March–July 1973. In fact, the practice of independent floating among LDC currencies was the exception during the
1970s and 1980s.[8] Most academic opinion opposed the LDCs'
practice of floating. They argued that LDC floating was either
not feasible or undesirable because of factors such as limited
capital markets, restrictions on capital flows and thin foreign exchange markets.[9] Only in the 1990s, under IMF tutelage, has
floating come into vogue for the LDCs and especially for the
countries in transition to market economies. Thirty-seven of the
48 countries that were independently floating in 1992 were either
LDCs or countries in transition.[10] However, the adoption of a
floating exchange-rate regime by these countries does not reflect
the LDCs' preference for a global system of flexible exchange
rates. Most LDCs have accepted a floating exchange-rate regime
as a requirement of an IMF stabilization program.

It is ironic, however, that many LDCs resorted to basket-pegging as a part of their search for stability on the seas of generalized
floating of major currencies. This very experience of working with
basket pegs provided the LDCs' monetary authorities with the ex-
pertise to deal with floating exchange rates. As explained above,
basket-pegging implies the destabilization of the individual exchange rates of a currency to the currencies in the basket. The
destabilization of the individual exchange rates was therefore an
introduction to generalized floating. The difference between basket-
pegging and general floating, however, is that with general floating
not even the effective exchange rate is stabilized. The Indian case is
representative of the increase in the variation of the exchange rate
of the domestic currency in terms of the intervention currency that
was introduced over the years in the operation of the basket peg. In
1976, the first full year of operation of the basket peg, the Reserve
Bank of India announced seven changes in the exchange rate of the
Indian rupee *vis-a-vis* the pound sterling, its intervention currency.
By 1983, the number of annual changes announced by the Bank
increased, gradually over the years, to 125.[11] Institutions needed to
be developed to deal with such continuous variations of the domestic currency *vis-a-vis* the intervention currency; these same institutions provided the basis for making a feasible transition to a fully
fledged float of the rupee.[12]

To sum up, the LDCs have realized that, in the absence of a global fixed exchange-rate regime, the second-best solution is pegging to a basket of currencies. It is not fixing to one of the so-called anchor currencies, which are themselves floating on the high seas of capital mobility. This realization, coupled with the ideologically oriented preference of the IMF for floating and convertibility, prompted many LDCs to switch to floating exchange rates as their authorities developed the skills and the institutions to handle floating exchange rates. This arrangement provided a free depreciation of their currency without having to take the responsibility for politically inexpedient decisions to devalue.[13] Nevertheless, the continued preference of the LDCs remains to be a global system of stable exchange rates.

Convertibility versus Floating

It is important, in this context, to distinguish between floating and convertibility: convertibility of currencies in the interest of increased world trade and global efficiency in the allocation of resources is one thing, market-determined floating exchange rates is another. The one can exist without the other. The Bretton Woods Charter emphasized convertibility (Article VIII obligations) with maintenance of par values (Article IV responsibilities). More recently, a separate distinction has been made between *soft* and *hard* convertibility:

> Soft convertibility entails the ability to freely exchange currencies *at market-determined exchange rates*, while hard convertibility entails the right to freely exchange currencies *at a given exchange rate*. By definition, soft convertibility applies to flexible exchange rate regimes, hard convertibility to fixed exchange rate regimes.[14]

Whether the opening up of the LDC economies and their increased participation in the world market system requires free convertibility of their currencies is debatable. This convertibility may not need to be at floating rates. If convertibility is a must, it can be *hard* rather than *soft* convertibility. The costs of exchange-rate flexibility – in terms of (a) its anti-trade bias and (b) the loss of a fixed exchange-rate anchor against inflation – are greater than the costs of restrictions on convertibility of currency.[15]

Fixed Exchange Rates and International Policy Coordination

What are the preconditions for a system of relatively stable exchange rates? The first requirement for maintaining exchange-rate stability is policy coordination among major countries.[16] The policy independence promised by a flexible exchange-rate regime is a myth. Policy coordination is necessary even in the context of the present system to avoid excessive volatility and exchange-rates misalignments. Successive Communiqués by the G–24 have called for such coordination in the interest of world financial stability. However, a chicken-and-egg relationship exists between macroeconomic policy coordination and exchange-rate stability: exchange-rate stability requires macroeconomic policy coordination but such coordination does not result from a strong desire for exchange-rate stability. Ronald McKinnon makes this point when he suggests that the international monetary system worked reasonably well in the late nineteenth century because countries pursued coordinated policies in defense of international gold parities.[17]

McKinnon has long advocated a return to the system of fixed exchange rates as a necessary condition for the very survival of a free-trade regime. The McKinnon standard would, of course, require a roughly common rate of inflation across countries; but the point is precisely that a commitment to fixed parities can yield the necessary monetary cooperation.

It may be useful to compare the McKinnon proposal of nominal parities with Williamson's target-zone proposal involving real parities. This latter proposal has been generally supported by the LDCs as a way to effect the view to bringing about policy coordination among major countries and stability in the exchange rates.[18] The recommendation of a Commonwealth Study Group under the Chairmanship of Prof. Gerald K. Helleiner is representative of the LDC support for the Williamson proposal:

> Just as under the original Bretton Woods exchange rate regime governments undertook to maintain the values of their currencies within an agreed band about their declared parities, under a target zone system they could commit themselves to intervention to the degree or at least in the direction required to maintain real effective rates broadly within the agreed zones.[19]

Like the McKinnon proposal, the Williamson proposal of target zones too is advocated on the grounds that a regime of unmanaged floating does not motivate countries to coordinate their economic policies. However, the Williamson proposal would maintain real, not nominal, exchange rates in broad zones – of as much as ten per cent – around the targeted level. This proposal would enable an accommodation of differential inflation rates between countries as well as the adjustment of terms of trade, by varying the real rate within the zone. This would yield a current account balance. McKinnon, on the other hand, believes that variations of exchange rates cannot achieve current account equilibrium: gains in competitiveness obtained through a devaluation trigger an increase in domestic real expenditure which offsets the initial improvement in the current account. McKinnon advocates sound fiscal policies to ensure current account equilibrium with fixed nominal exchange rates. This would equalize the price levels of internationally tradeable goods across countries during a period of substantial equilibrium of trade flows.[20]

Current Account versus Capital Account Convertibility

Volatile short-term capital flows are one of the most important constraints on the feasibility of introducing a system of relatively stable exchange rates, whether nominal or real. The demise of the Bretton Woods system has been attributed to large-scale capital mobility. Since then the problem of speculative capital flows has increased manifold. The dollar value of transactions in the world foreign-exchange markets is several times the dollar value of international trade in goods and services. Therefore, the first step toward exchange-rate stability is instituting international controls over short-term capital mobility. Such controls should be designed so that they do not adversely affect productivity-enhancing long-term capital flows. Tobin has advocated an internationally uniform transaction tax on foreign-exchange transactions with a view to 'throwing some sand in the well-greased wheels' of international financial market mechanisms.[21]

A suggestion by David Felix[22] to channel the proceeds of the tax to the LDCs through the IMF is worthy of consideration. Felix suggests two more measures to reduce the destabilizing effects of capital mobility on the developing economies: (a) using collaborative bank-supervisory mechanisms to reduce capital flight and tax evasion on foreign assets, and (b) using the exchange of tax-information agreements. These measures are possible within existing international institutions. What these measures require is an intellectual acceptance that some sands can be legitimately thrown in the wheels of the international financial-market mechanism in the larger interest of the financial stability necessary for development.

It should be noted that a distinction has always been made between convertibility on the *current account* (that is, currency transactions based on trade) and convertibility on the *capital account* (that is, currency transactions based on foreign investments or speculation). Further, while the IMF has always insisted on the former, the Fund's Articles of Agreement (see Article VI, Sections 1 and 3) explicitly allow controls on capital transactions. The Articles of Agreement (see Article IV, Section 4) also provide the adoption of a global regime based on stable but adjustable par values. These provisions could be exploited to move to a system of relatively stable exchange rates with the objectives of: (a) minimizing the effects of volatility and misalignments of exchange rates on the LDCs, and (b) promoting the international policy coordination required for better governance of an interdependent world. These could lead to the emergence, in the long run, of international institutions like a World Central Bank.

THE LEVEL OF LDC EXCHANGE RATES

The LDCs' promotion of floating and convertible exchange rates is organically linked with the currently fashionable insistence on devaluing LDC currencies. The former has indeed served as an instrument for the latter. The level at which the exchange rate is fixed is as important as the kind of exchange-rate arrangement. Under a fixed exchange-rate regime, an exchange rate may be fixed to produce an undervalued or overvalued currency. Similarly, a currency may depreciate or appreciate continuously under a flexible exchange-rate regime and still be misaligned all the time. Concern is mounting today on the IMF's emphasis on devaluing LDC currencies – a policy inconsistent with the exchange-rate stability emphasized by the Fund's Articles of Agreement.[23] Jeffrey Sachs speaks of a need for conceptual re-thinking in this context.[24] Proliferation of studies suggest that the period of overvalued LDC currencies broadly coincided with efforts by the international community to legalize the flexible

exchange-rate regime. The freedom *vis-a-vis* exchange arrangements afforded under the amended Articles provided an institutional set-up that made it easy to seek devaluations of LDC
currencies. Whereas only 30 per cent of the upper-credit tranche
programs between 1963 and 1972 included a devaluation, that
proportion rose to 50 per cent between 1977 and 1980 and to
nearly 80 per cent during 1983.[25] Jeffrey Sachs conjectures that
since 1980, the proportion of programs with devaluations has
been above 75 per cent of programs.[26] It should be noted that, in
addition to a heavy initial devaluation in the name of establishing
external competitiveness, the programs also involve a shift to a
more flexible exchange-rate regime to maintain competitiveness.
For example, the programs involved the adoption of a real
exchange-rate rule – that is, the targeting of the real exchange
rate – whereby the official nominal exchange rate is changed
frequently in order to take account of the difference between the
domestic and foreign rates of inflation.

Costs of Devaluation

The policy of large and continuous devaluations is promoted by
the myth that devaluations do not involve any real cost. However,
two aspects of this heavy emphasis on devaluation should be
noted, one relevant to small, relatively open, dependent economies, and the other relevant to large, relatively closed economies
with some 'market power'.[27]

In the case of small, open economies, a fixed exchange rate
can act as a nominal anchor against inflation. However, this
potential role for the exchange rate is lost when a regime resorts
to large and frequent devaluations in the name of maintaining
external competitiveness.[28] Montiel and Ostry exemplify this in
the case of countries which follow a real exchange-rate rule.[29]
Such a rule implies that the nominal exchange rate and the
money supply are both indexed to the domestic price level.[30]
Increases in the domestic price level are fully accommodated by a
faster exchange-rate depreciation and a faster monetary growth,
all of them implying real costs.

Conventional wisdom maintains that a devaluation may not
have any inflationary consequences in relatively closed large countries like India.[31] On the other hand, under assumptions which are
plausible in the case of such countries, devaluations will lead to a
substantial decline in the terms of trade, especially if the devalua-

tions are large, as was the case in recent years.[32] The argument for devaluations has been that they will create the export surplus needed to obtain a capital transfer to repay LDC debts. However, the argument ignored the negative effect on the terms of trade.

Devaluations also have other consequences which are fashionable to ignore. Devaluations lead to higher external debt-servicing obligations in terms of domestic currency. LDC governments who pay these debt-servicing obligations receive revenues which do not increase by devaluation. Thus, devaluations create higher fiscal deficits which are generally financed by printing money, leading to inflation and stimulating further devaluations.[33]

Appropriate Level of LDC Exchange Rate

The negative impacts of devaluations raise the question: what is the appropriate exchange-rate level that can be fixed for LDCs? The appropriate LDC exchange-rate level can be discussed in terms of two familiar concepts of the equilibrium exchange rate: Cassel's concept of the purchasing power parity (PPP), and Nurkse's concept of balance-of-payments equilibrium. In Cassel's view the equilibrium exchange rate between two currencies is the rate which satisfies the PPP. Nurkse explicitly rejected the PPP when he proposed the definition of the equilibrium exchange rate as the rate which, over a certain period of time, keeps the balance of payments in equilibrium:

> At the various monetary conferences after the last war, the late Gustav Cassel campaigned vigorously for the theory of 'purchasing power parity'. He and his followers were under the impression that this theory furnished all that was needed for the definition of equilibrium rate of exchange. Today it is realized that the purchasing-power-parity theory cannot provide a definition of equilibrium rate; that it can provide only a pseudo-definition in terms which themselves require definition and, indeed, turn out to be incapable of precise interpretation.[34]

Paul Samuelson and Bela Balassa have also criticized the PPP theory.[35] Yet the mainstream responses to the PPP theory are schizophrenic in two ways:

- Between the two versions of the PPP theory, the relative and the absolute, there exists a greater readiness to accept the relative version of the theory. The emphasis in IMF-supported adjustment programs on the adoption of real exchange-rate rules in LDCs indicates an intellectual acceptance of a relative PPP theory. Under such a rule the nominal exchange rate is managed so as to keep the real exchange rate from appreciating relative to some base period value. The base period itself is chosen on the basis of an actual equilibrium in the balance of payments with no pronounced cyclical factor at work. That is, the base period exchange rate is a Nurksian equilibrium rate.

- There is a greater readiness to accept the validity of the absolute version of the PPP theory for developed countries than for LDCs. For example, the law of one price for traded goods holds pretty well for the United States and Japan.[36] Modified versions of the PPP theory, for example the productivity-biased PPP theory, are proposed for LDCs.

There would be no problem in choosing between the theories when determining the appropriate level of exchange rate if the competing theories predicted, by and large, the same level of exchange rates. This is, however, far from true especially for the LDCs. The Nurksian rates for an equilibrium in LDCs' balance of payments are substantially lower than the PPP-determined rates. Beginning from the May 1993 issue of the *World Economic Outlook*, the IMF has changed its method of calculating the output shares of countries. It now uses the PPP-based exchange rates instead of the market-based dollar exchange rates for the conversion of individual country GDPs into a common denominator. This has substantially increased the share of world output accounted for by the developing countries (from 18 per cent to 34 per cent), with a corresponding decrease in the share of industrial countries (from 73 per cent to 54 per cent). It indicates the direction and the extent of deviation of the actual exchange rates from the PPP-based rates.

The criticism of the PPP theory, namely that it does not provide exchange rates which imply an equilibrium in the balance of payments, is well taken. There is, however, some merit to the view that the national currencies should bear some relationship to their purchasing powers across countries. This is especially true if the world is on its way to a common international currency. In an ideally integrated world, with productivity and other differences evened out between countries, for example, between sectors within countries, exchange rates would be determined on the basis of PPP. Thus, the PPP suggests some criteria. However, in the current situation, these criteria cannot be used to determine appropriate levels of LDC exchange rates, since that would lead to unsustainable balance-of-payments positions. The unsustainable balance-of-payments positions would necessitate restrictive policies in the LDCs which would, in turn, constrain their integration in the developed capitalist world.

Using the concept of the Nurksian equilibrium exchange rate there will be a deviation between this actual exchange rate and the PPP exchange rate. This deviation between the two rates could be used as one of the criteria in determining the 'compensation' payable to the LDCs to induce them to continuously integrate themselves into the developed capitalist system by adopting outward-looking policies inclusive of highly devalued exchange rates. These compensation payments are justified, since outward-looking policies with highly devalued exchange rates inflict real costs on LDCs. The mechanism for creating international liquidity could be used to pay this compensation to the LDCs. For example, purchasing power parity-weighted GDPs could be used instead of dollar exchange-rate-weighted GDPs in determining the LDCs' allotment of SDRs.

THE RESERVE STANDARD OF THE INTERNATIONAL MONETARY SYSTEM

Ideally the compensation would be in terms of the seigniorage that would result from the creation of an international asset. This asset would serve as a reserve asset, as a means of settling payments imbalances between countries, as a unit to fix the exchange rates of the national currencies and a unit of intervention by the central banks to maintain these rates.

SDR as an International Currency Unit

At various points in its *conception* the SDR has come close to being an international currency unit. However, the SDR as it exists in *actuality* has been the result of compromises, mainly among the developed world powers. Kindleberger speaks of five compromises that were necessary in creating the SDR.[37] These compromises in the creation of the SDR have robbed the SDR of much of its potential as an embryonic world monetary unit. The

SDR is today not even the 'principal reserve asset' of the world – a role propounded for it by the Committee of Twenty (C–20). The SDR merely serves as a unit of account in the IMF. It is important that the reform of the international monetary system should begin by allowing the SDR to play its due role in the system so that it evolves over the years towards a World Money Unit.

The Jamaica agreement and the subsequent amendments of the Articles of Agreement of the IMF provided the international community an opportunity to increase the status of the SDR as an international currency unit; but the opportunity was not seized. Thus the possibility of introducing the SDR for intervention purposes along the lines suggested in the Annex 3 of the 'Outline of Reform' of the C–20 has been lost for now.[38]

In the words of Benjamin Cohen:

> As a non-national currency, the SDR would by definition eliminate the sort of asymmetry that arises from the dollar's continuing position as universal intervention currency. What was required was the relaxation of the rule, under the original SDR agreement, limiting the SDR holdings to official monetary authorities only: if private financial institutions were also authorized to hold and trade SDRs, central banks could readily substitute SDRs for dollars in their intervention operations. But no such change was proposed at Jamaica.[39]

The role of the SDR as a reserve asset could also have been enhanced by the creation of a 'substitution account' to issue SDRs in exchange for outstanding dollar balances. Such an account would also have increased the ability of the United States to intervene jointly with other countries. Peter Kenen points out how the proposal was a non-starter:

> It was agreed in principle that the costs and benefits of the arrangements would be shared by the United States and the depositors, and Washington interpreted this understanding to mean that the depositors would bear some of any losses [that would occur if the dollar had depreciated in terms of the SDR over the lifetime of the account]. But other countries did not buy this interpretation, and discussions of this subject ended in 1980, when the United States shifted its own position, proposing that all losses be borne by the Fund, which would set aside some of its gold for the purpose.[40]

The SDR has been confirmed merely in its role as a unit of account because of the abolishing of the official price of gold and the valuation of the SDR in terms of a currency basket. The SDR's role as a *numeraire* for the system can, however, be greatly enhanced by using it to fix parities for currencies. This is not the same as using the SDR for expressing the flexible exchange rates as is currently the case. The SDR's role as a *numeraire* would imply introducing an SDR standard.[41]

The SDR Standard

Is it necessary that the value of such an SDR[42] be fixed in terms of, for example, gold as was the case when the SDR was first introduced? Alternatively, the issue of SDRs could be backed by gold or, more generally, by stocks of commodities. Mead's proposal, in which he talks in terms of Keynes' bancor instead of the SDR, is relevant in this context:

> To win acceptance the Bank might maintain the convertibility of bancor into gold, though not at a perpetually fixed rate, or it might seek to maintain its value against a basket of goods – a form of Tabular Standard proposed by Keynes and other economists during the interwar period and lately revived in circles as conservative as the *Wall Street Journal*.[43]

Such proposals for commodity-reserve standards have been advocated also by others.[44] A commodity standard can be criticized on two grounds: (a) it would be inflationary[45] or deflationary, depending on the supply of and demand for commodities and (b) the seigniorage associated with it would be substantially lower than that which could be obtained from fiduciary standards.[46] The creation of SDR without any backing in terms of gold or commodities, or even without any liability being assumed by the IMF, but merely through an agreement making SDRs acceptable to the central banks, is perhaps the single most important event in the post-war international monetary affairs. The myth of 'backing' has been finally exploded. It is in the fitness of things that the SDR continues to be a pure fiduciary standard. Substantial seigniorage benefits can be generated from the creation of international liquidity to be 'distributed consciously in accordance with any preconceived set of political or economic criteria'.[47]

A substantial seigniorage could be generated in the creation of

SDRs and distributed in favor of the LDCs.[48] There is, however, a dilemma in terms of the interest-rate charge on the SDR: an increase in the rate reduces the net benefit for those to whom SDRs are allocated; whereas a decrease in the rate reduces the attractiveness of holding SDRs as a reserve *vis-a-vis* other assets. Since 1974 the rate of interest paid on the holdings of SDR and the rate of charge levied on its use are determined by the market rate of interest. Hence, the seigniorage gained by the countries to whom the SDRs is allocated has been substantially diminished. It is important to note that the rate of interest available on the SDR should reflect the market rate of interest if the SDR were to be promoted in private portfolio and transaction use. This would be necessary in order to use the SDR as an intervention currency. Consequently, any scheme of SDR allocation in favor of LDCs will have to be in conjunction with an interest subsidy on the LDCs' use of SDRs.

CONCLUSION

The proposed exchange arrangements would have the following components:

- a system of relatively stable exchange rates on an SDR standard, with parities defined at appropriate levels and maintained to provide an anchor against inflation; and

- distribution of seigniorage benefits emerging from the SDR standard in favor of LDCs.

To make the system operational, it may be necessary to implement the following over a period of time:

- coordination of policies of the so-called anchor currency countries;

- promotion of the private use of SDRs with a view to developing a market for SDRs;

- fixing of parities of all currencies *vis-a-vis* the SDR such that even the major currencies are defined in terms of the SDR, reversing the present arrangement whereby the SDR is valued in terms of the major currencies;

- using the SDR market for intervention by central banks for the purpose of maintaining the parities of currencies; and

- allocation of SDRs explicitly in favor of LDCs with an interest subsidy to LDCs for the use of SDRs.

This arrangement could be the precursor to the introduction of a common world currency in the long run. In the medium term, it will support development by: (a) the financial stability it would promote, and (b) promoting the transfer of purchasing power to LDCs. The demand impulse necessary for world development and that Mead[49] talks of as being the core of Bretton Woods has to come from a fuller integration of the developing world into the world economy. The system proposed here would enable an equitable participation of LDCs in the world economy on terms which would be less unfavorable to the less developed countries.

Notes

1. The need for these world institutions has been brought out in United Nations Development Programme (UNDP), *Human Development Report 1992* (New York: Oxford University Press, 1992); and in Walter Russell Mead, 'American Economic Policy in the Antemillennial Era' in *World Policy Journal*, vol. 6/3 (Summer 1989) pp. 385–468. These two documents along with Howard M. Wachtel, *The Money Mandarins: The Making of a Supranational Economic Order*, revised edition (Armonk, NY: M.E. Sharpe, and London: Pluto Press, 1990), provided the vision for the Rethinking Bretton Woods project under which the present volume is published.
2. The adverse effects of the volatility and misalignments of major currencies on the LDCs have been well documented, especially by UNCTAD: United Nations Conference on Trade and Development (UNCTAD), *International Monetary Issues: The International Monetary System and Financial Markets, Recent Developments and the Policy Challenge* (Geneva: UNCTAD, 1984); United Nations Conference of Trade and Development (UNCTAD), *Compendium of Selected Studies on International Monetary and Financial Issues for the Developing Countries* (New York: United Nations, 1987); United Nations Conference on Trade and Development (UNCTAD), *International Monetary and Financial Issues for the 1990s: Research Papers for the Group of Twenty-Four*, vol. I to VI (New York: United Nations, 1993).
3. Committee on the Reform of the International Monetary System and Related Issues (Committee of Twenty), *International Monetary Reform: Documents of the Committee of Twenty* (Washington, DC: International Monetary Fund, 1974).

4. International Monetary Fund (IMF), *International Financial Statistics*, various issues (Washington, DC: IMF).

5. Continuing with the analogy of the seas of generalized floating, the pegging behavior of the LDCs reminds one of a Hindi saying: those prone to sinking will grab even a piece of straw for survival support.

6. These ideas were developed, among others, by Stanley W. Black, 'Exchange Rate Policy for Less Developed Countries in a World of Floating Rates' in *Essays in International Finance*, no. 119 (Princeton, NJ: Princeton University Press, 1976); and by William Branson and Louka Katseli-Papaefstratiou, 'Exchange Rate Policy for Developing Countries' in Sven Grassman and Erik Lundberg (eds), *The World Economic Order: Past and Prospects* (London: Macmillan, 1981) pp. 391–419. The relevant literature has been surveyed by John Williamson, 'A Survey of the Literature on the Optimal Peg' in *Journal of Development Economics*, vol. 11/1 (August 1982) pp. 39–61.

7. International Monetary Fund (IMF), *International Financial Statistics*, vol. 41/3 (March 1988) p. 20.

8. Only about ten of the 130 LDCs reported to practice of independent floating of their exchange rates, see, for example, International Monetary Fund (IMF), *International Financial Statistics*, vol. 41/3 (March 1988) p. 20.

9. Branson and Katseli-Papaefstratiou, 'Exchange Rate Policy for Developing Countries', p. 392.

10. International Monetary Fund (IMF), *International Financial Statistics*, vol. 46/3 (March 1993) p. 6.

11. The yearly changes in the exchange rate of the intervention currency announced by the Reserve Bank of India increased substantially in the subsequent years; but by then the Bank had adopted the policy of depreciating the Indian rupee against the basket and a large number of changes in the exchange rate were necessary to bring about this depreciation in a surreptitious fashion.

12. Interestingly, pegging to a basket of currencies was referred to by Black's influential article, 'Exchange Rate Policy for Less Developed Countries in a World of Floating Rates', as managed floating, the 'management' being of the intervention currency rate to maintain the effective exchange rate within the permitted bands producing a more or less continuous (depending on the width of the band) variation in the exchange rate of the intervention currency – a phenomenon akin to floating. This use of the term 'managed floating' is in contradiction with the use of the term by the IMF in its Table on Exchange Rate Arrangements where it refers to more flexible exchange rate arrangements including pegging to a basket (or even to a single currency) with wider margins or with the possibility of continuously adjusting the peg. Thus India was classified by the IMF as pegged to a currency composite up to January 1979 when its exchange rate was being determined with reference to a basket within a narrower margin of 2.25 per cent on either side of the parity; and subse-

quently as managed floating when the margin of pegging was increased to 5 per cent. In the IMF terminology, the management is of the exchange rate *vis-a-vis* the basket and not the intervention currency.

13. It should be noted that a decision to devalue would have to be explicitly made if the currency was pegged; whereas, under floating, devaluation can be attributed to the working of impersonal market forces. Under the reigning theory, such a devaluation, whether through an explicit decision under a fixed exchange-rate regime or through the market under-floating, would be required in order to reduce the trade deficit and/or to convert it into a trade surplus in order to be able to achieve a net outflow of capital for, for example, debt repayment in the case of highly indebted countries.

14. Report on a seminar paper by Manuel Guitian on 'Currency Convertibility: Concepts and Degrees' in *IMF Survey*, vol. 23/8 (April 18, 1994) p. 116.

15. The medium-term anti-trade bias of a flexible exchange-rate system has been brought out by Black, 'Exchange Rate Policy for Less Developed Countries in a World of Floating Rates'. The loss of nominal anchor is discussed in the next section in the context of excessive devaluation of LDC currencies under flexible regimes.

16. UNCTAD, *Compendium of Selected Studies* . . .

17. Ronald McKinnon, 'Monetary and Exchange Rate Policies for International Financial Stability' in *Journal of Economic Perspectives*, vol. 2/1 (Winter 1988) pp. 83–103.

18. John Williamson, 'Exchange Rate Management: The Role of Target Zones' in *American Economic Review*, vol. 77/2 (May 1987) pp. 200–4.

19. Gerald K. Helleiner, Conrad Blyth, Kenneth Dadzie, William Demas, Stuart Harris, Lal Jayawardena, Jeremy Morse, Harry M. Osha, Indraprasad G. Patel, *Towards a New Bretton Woods: Challenges for the World Financial and Trading System*, Report by a Commonwealth Study Group (London: Commonwealth Secretariat, 1983) p. 37.

20. The target-zone proposal of fixing real parities of major currencies can be used as a first step toward the ultimate fixing of nominal parities on an SDR standard as has been suggested below in Section III.

21. James Tobin, 'A Proposal for International Monetary Reform' in *Eastern Economic Journal*, vol. 4, no. 3–4 (July–October 1978) pp. 153–9. In the words of David Felix:

> As the uniform tax as a percentage of expected yield falls heaviest on 'short-term financial round-trip excursions into another currency,' and lightens the longer the foreign asset is held before the funds are repatriated, the tax would substantially reduce the post-tax profitability of short-term currency speculation while merely pinpricking foreign direct investment and other long-term capital flows.

David Felix, 'Suggestions for International Collaboration to Reduce Destabilizing Effects of International Capital Mobility on the Developing Countries' in United Nations Conference on Trade and Development (UNCTAD), *International Monetary and Financial Issues for the 1990s: Research Papers for the Group of Twenty-Four*, vol. III, (New York: United Nations, 1993) p. 57.

22. Felix 'Suggestions for International Collaboration...'
23. Article I (iii) enshrines as one of the purposes of the IMF to promote exchange-rate stability.
24. Jeffrey D. Sachs, 'Strengthening IMF Programs in Highly Indebted Countries' in Catherine Gwin and Richard E. Feinberg (eds), *The International Monetary Fund in a Multipolar World: Pulling Together* (New Brunswick, NJ: Transactions Books, 1989) p. 113.
25. Sebastian Edwards, 'The International Monetary Fund and the Developing Countries: A Critical Evaluation' in *National Bureau of Economic Research (NBER) Working Paper Series*, no. 2909 (Cambridge, MA: NBER, 1989); as reported in Sachs 'Strengthening IMF Programs in Highly Indebted Countries', endnote 27, pp. 121–2.
26. Sachs 'Strengthening IMF Programs in Highly Indebted Countries', endnote 27, pp. 121–2.
27. The term 'dependent economy' is used here in the Salter-Swan sense to denote those economies which take the price of tradeables on the world market as given and which consequently have no influence on their terms of trade; economies with 'market power' can influence their terms of trade.
28. The role of exchange rate as a nominal anchor against inflation has been discussed, for example, in W. Max Corden, 'Exchange Rate Policy in Developing Countries' in *Policy, Research, and External Affairs Working Papers*, WPS 412 (Washington, DC: World Bank, 1990).
29. Peter J. Montiel and Jonathan D. Ostry, 'Targeting the Real Exchange Rate in Developing Countries' in *Finance & Development*, vol. 30/1 (March 1993) pp. 38–40.
30. The money supply would be indexed to the domestic price level through the balance of payments since the real exchange rate is fixed.
31. The present author has, however, found evidence of the inflationary consequences of devaluation in the case of India. The anti-inflation argument against devaluation is, hence, also applicable for India.
32. Devaluations do not have terms-of-trade effects in the case of small dependent economies, since the prices of traded goods for small dependent economies are determined in foreign currency.
33. Devaluations have further negative consequences which are far from negligible. More work needs to be done to catalog the real costs of devaluation for different categories of LDCs.
34. Ragnar Nurkse, 'Conditions of International Monetary Equilibrium' in *Essays in International Finance*, no. 4 (Princeton, NJ: Princeton University Press, 1945).

35. Bela Balassa, 'The Purchasing Power Parity Doctrine: A Reappraisal' in *Journal of Political Economy*, vol. 72/6 (December 1964) pp. 584–96; Paul A. Samuelson, 'Theoretical Notes on Trade Problems' in *Review of Economics and Statistics*, vol. 46/2 (May 1964) pp. 145–54.

36. Lip service is paid to the absolute version of the PPP even in the case of LDCs. Thus, Montiel and Ostry explicitly define the PPP level of the real effective exchange rate as '*the level at which a unit of currency can buy the same bundle of goods in all countries*', Montiel and Ostry, 'Targeting the Real Exchange Rate in Developing Countries', p. 38, emphasis added.

37. Charles P. Kindleberger, 'The SDR as International Money' in Paul Coulbois (ed.), *Essais en l'honneur de Jean Marchal*, vol. 2: La Monnaie (Paris, Editions Cujas, 1975) pp. 303–14, reprinted in Charles P. Kindleberger, *International Money: A Collection of Essays* (London: George Allen and Unwin, 1981) pp. 63–75.

38. Committee of Twenty (1974) includes among others, the 'Outline of Reform' and accompanying Annexes of June 14, 1974; Annex 3 is on 'Exchange Margins and Intervention: Possible Operational Provisions with Illustrative Schemes'.

39. Benjamin J. Cohen, *Organizing the World's Money: The Political Economy of International Monetary Relations* (London: Macmillan, 1977) p. 127.

40. Peter B. Kenen, 'The Use of IMF Credit' in Catherine Gwin and Richard E. Feinberg (eds), *The International Monetary Fund in a Multipolar World: Pulling Together*, p. 87.

41. Fred Hirsch, 'An SDR Standard: Impetus, Elements, and Impediments' in *Essays in International Finance*, no. 99 (Princeton, NJ Princeton University Press, 1973).

42. Though we continue to use the term SDR, it will have to be replaced by a more appropriate term as the SDR grows to be a world monetary unit.

43. Mead, 'American Economic Policy in the Antemillennial Era', p. 433.

44. See, for example, Albert G. Hart, Nicholas Kaldor and Jan Tinbergen, 'The Case for an International Commodity Reserve Standard' in United Nations Conference on Trade and Development (UNCTAD), *Trade and Development*, vol. VIII: Miscellaneous Documents and List of Participants (New York: United Nations, 1964). See also the chapter by Bernard Lietaer in this volume.

45. See Charles P. Kindleberger, 'The Price of Gold and the N–1 Problem' in Charles P. Kindleberger (ed.), *International Money: A Collection of Essays* (London and Boston, MA: George Allen and Unwin, 1981) p. 78.

46. It is accepted, of course, that a commodity standard would have the beneficial effects of providing an efficient price and income support to the exporters of primary commodities.

47. Cohen, *Organizing the World's Money* . . ., p. 72.

48. A large number of schemes have been propounded to establish a link between SDRs and development finance. A paper prepared for the Committee of Twenty by the IMF Research Department classified the schemes into five types. The paper is reproduced in: Margaret Garritsen de Vries (ed.), *The International Monetary Fund 1972–1978: Cooperation on Trial*, volume III: Documents (Washington, DC: International Monetary Fund, 1985) pp. 69–97.
49. Mead, 'American Economic Policy in the Antemillennial Era', p. 396.

5 Global Currency Proposals

Bernard Lietaer

BACKGROUND

The national currencies of a few developed nations form the world's only liquid reserves and means of global exchange. A general consensus is now emerging that this has become detrimental to all parties. Dissatisfaction with the current system has been expressed in developing countries, particularly because of the different standards applied for reserve countries and for other nations. More recently, new factors have started to affect industrialized countries directly, creating an environment in which significant change is more likely. Among these new factors are:

- The current system has become unmanageable and unstable due to massive speculation (well over 90 per cent of all foreign exchange transactions are of a purely speculative nature, against less than 10 per cent for all investments and trade for goods and services around the world).

- In addition, the role of reserve currency and medium of exchange in the global economy is now backfiring on the countries involved. When Zaire wants to trade with Argentina or India, it has to do it in US dollars, and those US dollars can only be earned by directly or indirectly exporting to the United States. Hence, there is a structural and global pressure on the reserve countries to import more than their own interests dictate.

- There is also an increasing loss of control by the reserve currency countries on their own monetary policy. Private Japanese bond managers and non-US Central Banks together have larger holdings in US government securities than the Federal Reserve itself, thereby dwarfing the Reserve's intervention means.

- The new requirements of the transition economies (the economies of the former Communist world) were never part of the design of the Bretton Woods system, and are therefore not being met.

- Business considers now that foreign-exchange risks dwarf all other 'normal' business risks, and many foreign investments are not made simply because the currency risk is too high or too expensive to cover.

For the first time in half a century, the time is realistically ripe for a concrete proposal for a new monetary system that could actually be implemented. Several proposals have been made toward replacing the current system with a new global currency, a currency in addition to national currencies.

THREE TYPES OF GLOBAL CURRENCIES

A Global Fiat Currency

This currency would be created by a reformed International Monetary Fund (IMF) without any external reference. The Special Drawing Rights (SDRs) are an example of such a currency, but the SDRs are in fact based on a basket of national currencies. The new global fiat currency would not be based on such a basket. It would require management by the reformed IMF to prevent excessive issuance and to relate it to the needs of global economic activity.

A major advantage of such a currency is that it is very flexible in terms of the amounts issued, and is most familiar to today's monetary experience. This flexibility of issuing fiat currency in any quantity also has a potential drawback, noted already by Ricardo in 1817: 'Experience, however, shows that neither a State nor a Bank ever had the unrestricted power of issuing paper money, without abusing that power.'[1] However, the main problem with such a global fiat currency is that it does not provide any structural link to the 'real' economy. It would just provide an additional currency against which the global speculation could play. As it has no intrinsic value, it therefore does not provide any greater real standard of value than any national fiat currency does. This was already recognized by Hogart and Pearce, when they stated that:

> It will not be long before the world comes to recognize anew that it is no more possible to conduct affairs without a proper standard of value than it would be to conduct affairs without an agreed unit of length or weight.[2]

A Commodity-Valued Global Reference Currency

The value of a commodity-valued global currency could be determined by a basket of a dozen key commodities. Since the value of the currency refers to the value of a basket of goods, the currency could also be called a reference currency, differing from a fiat currency whose value does not refer explicitly to any good or basket of goods. For historical and psychological reasons, gold should be one of the commodities in the basket. The other eleven commodities could be the most traded commodities in the global markets. The weighting of these twelve commodities in the basket could be based on a 5-year moving average value as they are traded in the global markets. The selection of the eleven non-gold commodities could be revised periodically, for example every ten years, to ensure that the basket includes the most traded commodities. The resulting change in the value and composition of the basket would thus secure a stable but evolutionary reference value.

The major advantages of this reference currency are that the reference currency provides a link with the real world, and that it formally introduces the raw-materials producers (many of which are from transition economies or developing countries) into the global currency system. In many cases, commodities are associated with instability, but while this is true for any individual component, the overall stability would be ensured by the diversity of the basket of about twelve commodities. Such a basket is definitely more stable than any individual currency today. Furthermore, should any particular commodity experience a major price change (for example, the oil crisis of the 1970s), the value of the global currency itself would adjust and therefore dampen the global inflationary impact.

The major disadvantage of the purely commodity-*valued* currency is that it does not include a commodity *backing* of the currency. Some people claim that such a backing is a step backwards to a more primitive form of exchange. In fact, exactly the opposite may be true:

> From a practical point of view, commodity money is the only type of money that, at the present time, can be said to have passed the test of history in market economics. Except for short interludes of war, revolution, and financial crisis, Western economies have been on commodity money systems from the dawn of their history almost up to the present time. More precisely, it is only since 1973 that the absence of any link to the commodity world is claimed to be the normal feature of the monetary system. It will take several decades before we can tell whether the Western world has finally embarked, as so often is claimed, on a new era of non-commodity money or whether the present period will turn out to be just another interlude.[3]

Indeed, in the 1970s, we have experienced, in the monetary system as a whole, the biggest global inflation run-up in modern history; in the 1980s, a traumatic strangulation of the developing countries by external debt; and in the 1990s, speculative activity in currencies without historical precedent. If there is a consensus on the global economic evolution since we moved into the world of non-commodity money, it is around the word 'uncertainty'.

A Commodity-Backed Global Reference Currency

This particular global currency adds two features to the previous proposal. First, the global currency would not only be *valued* but also fractionally *backed* by a buffer stock of the dozen commodities in the basket. Thus, the buffer stock would not only enhance the stability of the currency but also provide a new tool for the global community to reduce the impact of disasters and other shocks. The size of the buffer stock would be determined in terms of a desirable number of weeks or months of world consumption, and the amount held as a fraction of total outstanding currency would be reviewed periodically.

Second, the costs of creating and maintaining this buffer stock would be charged to the holders of the global reference currency. This key feature stimulates the use of the currency as a medium of exchange, while discouraging using it as a store of value. This charge on the holders of the currency creates automatically what has been variously described in the Anglo-Saxon literature as *stamp scrip* or *stamp currency*; and by *Wara* (merchandise currency) or *Freies Geld* (free money) in the German literature.

The theoretical concept of a stamp scrip was originally developed by Silvio Gesell[4] during the latter part of the last century. Silvio Gesell was an Argentine businessman and economist who has been neglected by many theoretical economists because of the – at first sight – unconventional nature of his 'charge' concept, technically called 'demurrage'. His starting premise is that money as a medium of exchange is considered a public-service good (just as public transportation, for instance), and therefore a small user fee is levied on it. Instead of receiving interest for holding such a currency, the bearer is in fact paying interest. In Gesell's time, stamps were the normal way to levy such a charge. Now, the generalized use of computers in payment and accounting systems, as well as the availability of electronic debit cards ('smart cards') would make this procedure much easier and convenient to implement than ever before, without the inconvenience of handling any physical stamps.

Is such an unconventional concept as Gesell's 'charge money' a theoretically sound one? The answer is a resounding yes, and is supported by personalities of no lesser stature than John Maynard Keynes. Chapter 17 of Keynes' *General Theory of Employment, Interest and Money* analyzes the implications of such money, and provides a solid theoretical backing to the claims made by Gesell. He specifically states that:

> Those reformers, who look for a remedy by creating artificial carrying cost for money through the device of requiring legal-tender currency to be periodically stamped at a prescribed cost in order to retain its quality as money, have been on the right track, and the practical value of their proposal deserves consideration.[5]

Keynes concluded with the amazing statement that 'the future would learn more from Gesell than from Marx'.[6] The best recent contemporary analysis of Gesell's thesis is provided by Suhr.[7] He also provides solid answers to some of the criticisms levied against it. In addition, Hajo Riese[8] makes the point that the usual positive interest-bearing money creates systematic sub-optimization in capital allocations. Other economists who have studied the theoretical and practical implications of such alternative currencies include: Cohrssen, Dahlberg, Fisher, Herr and Yeager.[9]

IMPLICATIONS OF A COMMODITY-BACKED
GLOBAL CURRENCY

The simple process of charging the holder of the currency over time has a significant impact on behavior patterns. It provides an incentive to separate the currency's function as a medium of exchange from its function as a store of value. Commingling these two functions of money has become a habit only over the past 200 years. For instance the word capital itself comes from the Latin '*capus, capitis*' referring to the head of cattle (as still used in Texas: 'He is worth 1000 head.').

At first sight, it seems to be convenient that money is also a store of value. However, there is a formidable hidden cost in this convenience since the additional function of money as a store of value significantly exacerbates the business cycle and has other side-effects best revealed by describing the positive aspects of separating the two functions of money.

Impact on the Business Cycle

The reason is explained by the theory of time preference of money, which describes the rational trade-off between consumption today versus saving for the future. When someone expects higher uncertainty in the future, a larger proportion of that person's wealth is logically kept as savings against these uncertainties, and automatically a lower percentage used for immediate consumption. Therefore, at the first signs of a recession, anybody who has money will logically save more and consume less, thereby exacerbating the recession for everybody else. Similarly, in boom years, consumer optimism prevails, and people will simultaneously tend to dip into their savings to buy big-ticket items such as cars and houses, thereby pushing the boom into an inflationary period.

While other factors obviously also play a role in the creation of business cycles, it has been demonstrated many times that psychological effects, like consumer confidence, significantly exacerbate the problem. With the proposed system, this boom/bust tendency would be significantly reduced, because the demurrage charge implies a separation of money as a medium of exchange from money as a store of value.

Impact on Employment

The immediate effect of a charge currency is a strong incentive to avoid hoarding in this currency: people prefer to invest or spend it on goods or services and thereby generate a chain reaction of economic transactions which otherwise would either occur in a much slower fashion, or simply not occur at all. This means, in practice, a strong and immediate creation of local employment without the need for government intervention.

This positive effect on employment is also possible to explain by using Fisher's classical equation (also known as the quantity theory of money): $MV = PQ$, where M is the stock of money, V is velocity of turnover of money, P is the price level and Q is the overall volume of output or income. The demurrage charge implies that the velocity of money increases, since people don't like to hoard the charge currency. On the other hand, since the price level is fixed to the price of the basket of commodities, it has to be the case that output increases similar to the increase in velocity.

During the 1930s, most of the real-life implementations of 'stamp scrip' were aimed at specifically reducing unemployment: in all the cases where it was correctly implemented this objective was met with complete success, as some examples later in this chapter illustrate.

The implementation of current technologies has generated a new phenomenon of 'jobless growth' in the developed world. In Europe, unemployment has reached alarming levels. In the United States, the displacement of jobs from traditional manufacturing and white-collar activities has occurred to jobs in other sectors, most of which are lower paying. In the developing countries, unemployment and underemployment have a much longer history and have never really been solved in the previous system. Therefore, the issue of structural employment on a global level promises to become more rather than less critical in the future. Implementing a commodity-backed global currency would be the most powerful structural incentive to counteract structural unemployment.

Impact on Inflation

Furthermore, if used correctly, such a currency helps to push inflation down. Inflation is simply the depreciation of a currency in terms of goods. The proposed currency has an impact on two sides.

First, while inflation reduces the value of a currency over time, a charge currency becomes automatically more valuable over time. Such a currency acts in this respect as any other commodity which has a significant storage cost: it increases in value over time. (Today's future markets in gold, for instance, show in practice always a higher future value than the spot price, reflecting precisely such a cost of storage over time.)

Second, there is a substantial 'interest cost' built into every good and service purchased. Margrit Kennedy calculates that even in a relatively low-interest country such as Germany, the average interest component in the cost of garbage collection reaches 12 per cent, for drinking water 38 per cent, for sewage costs 47 per cent, and for social housing a whopping 77 per cent.[10] By eliminating interest costs from the economy, the actual cash outlay required for any given good or service would be dramatically reduced.

Impact on Ecology

The most recent reason for interest in stamp scrip and similar alternative monetary systems in the West or in Japan results from environmental concerns:[11]

> The higher the money-rate of interest, the higher is the pressure on entrepreneurs to avoid internal costs, that is, to externalize into the environment as much of the cost as is possible. Thus under neutral money, when interest goes to zero, this additional burden on resources will cease.[12]

This would be even more true with the commodity-backed global currency, where interest rates attain negative values. When it pays more to cut a tree, sell the wood and let the proceeds earn interest than simply let the tree grow, it is predictable that more trees will be cut than is optimal from an ecological viewpoint.

The most important structural shifts would occur in the way people would spontaneously start saving, investing and consuming. The demurrage concept discourages the use of currency as a saving device. If such currencies come into widespread use, the question which arises is what one can use to store value.

The conceptual key to understand this shift involves changing the 'arrow of time' in the investment process. Under the present system, the discounted present value of any investment has to be higher than the interest rate of a risk-less government bond. This implies that anything that produces value more than 20 years in the future is basically discounted as worthless today. This provides a systemic incentive not to care about the long-term future consequences of our actions, including environmental degradation, for instance. Under the proposed system, the incentive works, in fact, in the opposite way since income in the future would become more valuable than income today, thereby pushing the attention towards long-term implications of current actions.

Once the basic necessities of life are covered, the logical actions include the following:

- Invest in ways that will reduce expenses in the future: pay back mortgages, improve home insulation, improve energy efficiencies, start food gardens.

- Invest in anything that will at the very least keep, or better, increase in value in the future: land improvements, trees and forests and anything that grows over time. If one wanted to prepare a nest egg for grandchildren's college, instead of opening a savings account, one logical thing to do would be to plant, for example, a small forest.

- New liquid forms of savings would immediately develop as well, as soon as the demand for liquidity in the fixed assets just mentioned above would expand, for example, stock would be issued in companies that plant trees.

- In general, stocks would be preferred to bonds, thereby making access to investment capital at low leverage the dominant way of financing businesses.

- Consumption patterns would evolve towards products with a longer lifetime. For example, assume that one has $100,000 available and two types of cars are offered for sale: a car which costs $20,000 and lasts about 8 years (as in the current market), and one which costs $50,000 and lasts 20 years. In today's currency environment, it is logical to buy the short-lived car (because the $30,000 balance can be put in a savings account and get more value in the long run). With the proposed currency, however, it is logical to buy the long-lived car. Today, no company builds a car like that, because there is no demand for it. In the future, it would become the type of car in the highest demand. Notice that in the example provided, total income of the car manufacturer is the same over 20 years (assuming no inflation), but the burden on the environment is much lower in the second case.

- Based on the same logic, people would tend to build houses that would last as long as possible, and whenever they have some extra cash available they would spontaneously invest in further insulation and other improvements.

It is important to realize that in all the above examples, there was no need to provide tax incentives or otherwise induce people to do all these things: financial self-interest directly would provoke such actions. This is the reason for calling this particular global currency a 'green' global reference currency.

Today, certain groups try to convince others to act in an ecologically responsible way, while it is in their financial interest to do the opposite. With the proposed system, the economic self-interest pulls automatically in the direction of ecologically sound actions. Only by such realigning of the economic and moral motivations can truly massive changes in behavior patterns be expected. As will be shown later, whenever the currency of the realm had a built-in demurrage, these behavior patterns did indeed materialize.

Impact on International Business

Textbooks may claim that businesses are competing for markets and resources, but in fact it is clear that businesses really compete for money, using markets and resources. (The proof is that whenever a particular market is not profitable, business will legitimately move to another activity in another market.) So, a proposal for a new commodity-backed global currency is in fact a redesign of the objective for which the international corporations are competing. It is therefore essential to assess why business would be interested in using the proposed currency, and how its introduction would make an impact on international operations.

First of all, why should business be interested in using the proposed commodity-backed currency in the first place? The short answer is that the stability in the value of such a currency makes it an ideal forecasting and contract currency, particularly for medium- to longer-term planning or contracts (in practice more than three years). This would make it possible to structurally eliminate from contracts the currency risks which are currently so detrimental to reliable business planning. Although business – like any other profit-based entity – would not be interested in saving in this currency, it could be easy to buy it in the market whenever needed for payments as well. One could also simply express any values in contracts in the new currency, but at the moment of payment compute the corresponding amounts in any national currency including the US dollar and make the actual payments in such a national currency (as is currently often the practice in Europe with ECU-denominated contracts).

There is also a strategic reason why the introduction of such a currency is a good idea from the business perspective. By using this currency – as was noted earlier – the financial interests of business are realigned with ecological sustainability. The pressure for regulations would therefore be structurally less important over time, simply because they would be less necessary. More than today, it would become in the direct financial interest of the corporations to do what is sustainable in the long run anyway.

Finally, the issue of the interests of the banking sector itself should be addressed. As stated in the first section of this chapter, less than ten per cent of all foreign-exchange transactions involve the exchange of goods and services. This is the only part that the commodity-backed currency would be involved in. Well over 90 per cent of all foreign-exchange transactions would not be affected at all by this proposal. In addition, it should, of course, not be expected that all international business transactions would suddenly become denominated in this new currency, so the real percentage of transactions which would remain as now would be closer to 95 per cent. Finally, there is no reason why the banking sector would not charge the usual spread between bid and ask in transactions denominated in the new currency.

The four objectives – stabilizing the business cycle, spontaneous creation of employment, inflation control and ecologically sustainable growth – are results that economists can predict from the introduction of this commodity-backed global currency. However, the proof is in the pudding. Even more persuasive than any theoretical discussion is compelling evidence from case histories: such systems have indeed been used in the past in a variety of cultures, sometimes for centuries, and have always had the impact mentioned above.

SOME HISTORICAL PRECEDENTS

'Charged' currency is part of the Western inheritance with a much longer history than generally perceived. The oldest-known historical precedent is Egypt, where such a system was integral to a prosperity lasting more than one thousand years. Remember the biblical Joseph who saved Egypt from 'the seven lean years' announced in Pharaoh's dream? Why did the Egyptians keep Joseph in such high regard simply for inventing stockpiling, which must have existed in some form or another in most primitive hunter–gatherer tribes? Or was there something more to his system than that?

What the Bible fails to mention is that these stockpiles were also used as the basis for the currency system. Each farmer who contributed to the stockpile obtained a warehouse receipt – usually a piece of broken pottery with the inscription of the date and the quantity of bags of wheat he had contributed. They are the 'ostraca', thousands of which have been unearthed all over Egypt. The key to it, however, was a time charge on these receipts – to pay for the guardian of the depot, and to compensate for the pilferage by rodents – constituting the 'demurrage' of the Gesell money. This currency remained in use in Egypt until it was forcibly replaced by the Roman currency during the late Ptolemaic period.[13] Is it a coincidence that from that time on, and to this day, the economic 'miracle of the Nile' has never recurred?

Other interesting precedents of successfully using charge currencies as the dominant legal tender for an extended period of time occurred in Europe. What generated the extraordinary economic prosperity in Europe from 1150 to 1350? What enabled, for instance, the construction of the cathedrals, all built in that time interval, as well as the creation of some of the most lasting and interesting art works of its history? At least part of the answer lies in the currency of the time, called 'brakteaten'. They were metallic plaques, usually of cheap metal with a seal of the local authority, which were regularly recalled and replaced with new ones (in some instances yearly or even quarterly). But in this process a tax was levied called 'seigneurage' (up to 30 per cent of the value of the previous issue!). This tax was a significant source of income to the local lord. It also amounted to a substantial effective demurrage fee.

No wonder people preferred to invest in tapestries, paintings or even cathedrals rather than hoard currencies.[14] After all, the cathedrals – besides their important symbolic and religious value – also played the economic role of today's Disneyland, by attracting pilgrims to the city. In other words, they were a grandiose way to create future income to the community as a whole. It is also significant that – in contrast to their modern counterparts – they were built to last forever.

More recently, and even more directly relevant to our proposal, are the variety of practical monetary experiments carried out in the West during the depression of the 1930s. Three of these examples will be discussed here.

One further example focuses on the economy of the small town of Schwanenkirchen in Bavaria, which had been wiped out (as was the rest of Germany) by the hyperinflation and economic recession of the 1920s. The owner of the bankrupt local coal mine, Mr Hebecker, decided in a desperate effort to propose payment to his workers not in Reichsmark, but directly in *Wara*, payable in coal from the mine. Each *Wara* was issued on a par with the Reichsmark, and on the reverse side dated spaces were printed. Each month the bearer of the *Wara* bill had to purchase a stamp at a cost of one per cent of the face value in order for this particular bill to remain valid. This was justified as a 'storage cost for the coal backing the bill'. The workers paid for their food and local services with this currency. The baker in turn explained to his wheat suppliers that the only way he could pay them was in that same currency. The wheat suppliers and equipment manufacturers at the end of the cycle simply ended up redeeming the bill for coal from Mr Hebecker's mine.

Schwanenkirchen became quickly the most prosperous community in Bavaria. By 1931, this 'Freiwirtschaft' ('free economy') movement had successfully spread throughout Germany, involving no less than 2000 corporations and a variety of commodities in the *Wara* exchange system. Unfortunately, this experiment was blocked by the Central Bank in November 1931, and continuing economic stagnation generated the general dissatisfaction which brought to power Adolf Hitler with the well-known consequences.

In 1932, Austria was also in the middle of its deepest depression. Unemployment was reaching over 30 per cent and the central government could not do much to help. The mayor of the town of Wörgl, Mr Unterguggenberger, decided to copy the Schwanenkirchen example. He convinced the town hall to issue 14,000 Austrian shillings in 'stamp scrip' covered by the same amount of ordinary Austrian shillings deposited in a bank. This money again was valid only if each month one applied a stamp to its back, corresponding to the charge rate applicable to this currency. Two years later, Wörgl became, just as Schwanenkirchen in Germany, the most prosperous town in Austria. Taxes were paid early, the water supply and the paved road system extended all over town, inhabitants had repaired and repainted their homes, forests had been cleaned, trees were planted, a new bridge had been built. (This bridge still exists, and a plaque commemorating its construction with stamp scrip is still in place today.)

No less than 200 cities of Austria decided to imitate Wörgl. At this point the Central Bank of Austria felt threatened in its monopoly of currency emission and blocked the extension of the system against the opinion of the vast majority of the population. This decision was appealed all the way to the Austrian Supreme Court but was upheld.

The third example of stamp scrip in the 1930s could have been the biggest experiment of all. In the United States, Dean Acheson, then Assistant Secretary of the Treasury, was approached by Professor Irving Fisher with the same idea under the name of 'stamp scrip'. One feature of Professor Fisher's approach was that the 'charge' stamp was fairly high (two per cent per week) and was calculated so that the face value would be amortized over one year, and the currency withdrawn at that point.

Acheson decided to have the whole concept verified by his economic advisor, the well-respected Professor Russel Sprague, of Harvard University. The answer was that indeed stamp scrip would work perfectly economically, but that it had some implications for decentralized decision making which Acheson should verify in Washington. By this time, the 'stamp scrip movement' as it became known, had spread to 450 cities around the United States. For example, the city of St Louis, Missouri, had decided to issue $100,000 worth of stamp money.

Similarly, Oregon was planning to launch a $75 million stamp scrip issue. A federal law had been introduced in Congress by Congressman Pettengil of Indiana to issue $1 billion of stamped currency. In 1933, Irving Fisher, Hans Cohrssen and Herbert Fisher published a little handbook entitled *Stamp Scrip* for practical management of this currency by communities, and described the actual experience of 75 American communities with it.[15]

Just at that time, however, on March 4, 1933, Roosevelt announced the New Deal. It announced the temporary closing of all banks, prohibited the issue of 'emergency currencies', and launched a series of centrally determined 'public work projects'.

The last example is the only case known where this kind of

currency is still legal tender today. On the island of Guernsey, part of the United Kingdom, it was originally introduced as an emergency currency during the Napoleonic Wars, and evolved to permanent legal tender after 1914. The economic impact of these wars was unusually harsh on the Channel Islands, including Guernsey. Invoking an ancient prerogative to produce its own notes, in 1813 Guernsey issued 4000 Guernsey pounds which were interest free. While this experiment was not strictly using demurrage, it did clearly go a long way in that direction compared to a 'normal' interest environment. Within months local community projects included repairing buildings and roads, and later on rebuilding Elizabeth College. Issues were made with great care to avoid inflation. The islanders considered the success so effective that this interest-free currency is still used today. British respect for historic precedent made it possible for this experiment to continue. The results are also still visible today: from a small poor island without resources, the island has become very prosperous, and can afford to levy very low taxes on its inhabitants.[16]

One can conclude, therefore, that whenever 'charge currencies' have been used in practice, whether as an 'emergency currency' or as normal long-term legal tender, economic prosperity has been the result. More specifically, its initial impact is a strong growth in the economy including an increase in employment, a gradual lowering of costs (as the interest component built into the prices of all goods and services is eliminated), and in the longer run a stable and sustainable growth. The modern experiments were blocked not because they were unsuccessful, but paradoxically because their very success was perceived as threatening to centralized decision making.

SOME POTENTIAL MISUNDERSTANDINGS

The concepts presented here may prompt some questions about classical economic concerns. Keynes commented in this context: 'The difficulty lies, not in the new ideas, but in escaping from the old ones, which ramify, for those brought up as most of us have been, into every corner of our minds.'[17]

Savings and Investments

What happens to savings and investments under such a global currency regime? With a reduction in the propensity to hoard currency, one could conclude that savings disappear. According to the classical equation, 'savings equal investments', the latter would similarly be reduced.

The fallacy in the above argument lies in assuming that cash, saving accounts and similar cash equivalents are the only form that savings can take. People would indeed save less in these forms of monetary assets, but would save more in real physical assets, including productive assets. The more creative banks would immediately provide a way to create liquid forms of investments in such assets. These new savings accounts, which would enable small withdrawals and additions to a very conservative form of mutual fund invested in equity investments in assets, with growing value over time, would become the norm.

Large-scale projects could be financed, as today, by issuing stock, which would become in fact more valuable (and therefore easier to sell) than in a 'normal' market economy, because it represents promises of future cash flows. One can have a taste of this phenomenon in today's stock markets: whenever interest rates drop, the stock markets boom. Similarly, bonds could still be issued, but their interest rate would be much lower than today. It is likely that the proportion of financing due to equity versus bonds would increase compared to today, because at present interest is tax-deductible while dividends are not. As the current practice has been often criticized because it creates higher leverage and therefore more instability in business overall, this feature is in fact an additional positive implication for the proposed system. All other things being equal, one should even expect a net increase in total investments after introducing charge currency, but the forms these investments would take would be different.

Inflationary Behavior

The behavior of shunning currency is very similar to what is observed under inflation. So is this not another form of inflationary behavior?

While the behavior patterns generated by the demurrage concept do indeed look similar to what is observed under inflation, the cause is different. Just as one can have a group of people streaming out of a room because of a fire inside or because a celebrity is outside, observed behavior is very similar, but the causes and consequences are not the same. The incentive to spend the money because of demurrage is structurally different from avoidance of inflated currency. More important, the consequences are also diametrically opposed: under hyperinflation, social structures collapse; while with demurrage currencies the fabric of society is reinforced.

In technical terms, this misunderstanding results from a failure to distinguish between a depreciation of the purchasing power of the monetary unit (that is, inflation), and the devaluation solely of the means of payment while the unit of measurement remains stable (that is, demurrage money). This important distinction has been clarified by Langelutke and also by Suhr.[18]

In the case of inflation, people cannot escape the carrying charges of money by obtaining claims to future money such as bonds, whose unit of measurement remains stable. Bond prices collapse, because interest rates have to climb higher still than the inflation rate. These high-interest rates further strangle the economy in the process. In addition, trust in the entire economic structure is lost by the unstable value of the monetary unit itself.

None of these problems appear with charge-rate currency. Bonds and any other forward claims to future money become in fact more valuable because they represent a way to avoid the penalty of holding cash. Real interest rates drop. The value of the monetary unit itself remains stable, guaranteeing to all economic agents access to transaction money at low and predictable costs.

Banking and Capital Rationing

How is banking and capital rationing possible in a demurrage currency environment? Let us assume that the charge rate charged to the public at large on bills and savings accounts is a negative two per cent. The banks themselves would be charged a slightly lower percentage on their own funds (for example, a negative one per cent) in order to provide them similarly with incentives not to hoard their reserves. Finally, banks would still be able to lend out in a free market for housing or other creditworthy project loans at a low, but positive rate, such as one or two per cent for instance.

Therefore, banks can still have their normal spreads between the cost of funds and the market interest rates, and market rationing would still operate. The only significant difference from the current interest-rate structure is that the starting point is a negative two per cent instead of, for instance, six per cent in the United States today.

There is another relevant aspect from the traditional bank viewpoint: many banking specialists have indeed pointed out that disintermediation is a growing threat to the traditional banking role. It is also well known that such disintermediation always increases dramatically whenever the interest rates reach high levels. It is logical that the temptation to short-cut the bank is highest when direct investments in government bills become more attractive.

Banks in the proposed system are ideally placed to become the suppliers and packagers of the new forms of liquid savings described earlier. An ideal savings account would in fact become a specialized form of low risk mutual fund management. Since government bonds would be yielding extremely low returns, the threat of disintermediation in this role would be further reduced.

Demurrage and Buffer-Stock Costs

What would happen to the funds raised with the demurrage charge? First of all, if the issued global currency is backed at 100 per cent of the value of the buffer stocks, the funds raised would directly serve to pay the costs of creating and maintaining the buffer stocks over time, for all the commodities of the basket. As the demurrage charge is computed to exactly cover these costs, this system could work indefinitely. This would also be the recommended way to start off this new system, since it would also give maximum credibility to this new currency.

If after a few years of successful use it is desired to expand the use of this global currency, one could decide to have only fractional coverage by the commodity basket. The reasoning is the same as in current banking: the likelihood that the whole amount of the global currency will need to be redeemed against commodities at the same time is almost nil. One can therefore afford to have only a fractional coverage. In this case, there are two choices how to operate the system:

- the institution issuing the reference currency can simply reduce the demurrage charge to reflect the lower costs of backing the global currency; or

- the institution issuing the reference currency can keep the charge at its initial level, thereby creating a net income flow for the issuing institution, consisting of the demurrage charge which is not needed to cover the cost of the buffer stock. The use of this predictable and steady income flow is again a decision which is open.

For instance, the issuing institution which receives the net income flow could create a sinking fund. This fund could be used to buy back the reference currency from the public at the discretion of the issuing institution. This implies that the reference currency once issued can be withdrawn and does not need to circulate forever. This was the process recommended by Fisher in the 1930s for the stamp scrip issues he planned in the United States. Hence, the issuing institution is able to fine-tune the amount of reference currency circulating in the economy. If it is considered not desirable to withdraw the reference currency, the issuing institution can simply opt for a new issue.

Alternatively, if considered desirable, the issuing institution could use the global income from the global currency for financing selected global institutions, such as the United Nations, or other activities of global interest, thereby relieving nation states of the burden of financing these activities.

The system of a reference currency leaves open these choices, as the benefits presented earlier for it remain valid independently of the use of the proceeds of the global currency demurrage charges. It is ultimately a political decision on how best to use this potential new global income.

CONCLUSION

It is very rare in anyone's lifetime to have the opportunity to rethink a new monetary system. It is also an issue that may affect generations from all cultures in the future. There are still monetary specialists, as well as ecologists, who do not see the direct impact that monetary systems have on the 'invisible hand' of ecologically sustainable activity. There may still be people who believe that monetary systems are mostly a technical matter which affect only some rarefied circles of high finance. At the end of the twentieth century, with the collapse of the Communist system and the move of China towards a money-based motivation system, the next monetary system will be the first in recorded history to affect the entire human species simultaneously.

Just one example: the Chinese are planning to emit by 2010 as much carbon dioxide into the atmosphere as the entire planet emits today. However complacent one may be about today's environmental degradation, it is obvious that in the foreseeable future something will have to be done, or irreversible climate or other changes will oblige us to do so. What ways do we have to influence the decisions of one billion Chinese, other than a global monetary system? Those in charge of designing the next monetary system should be aware that we may not have another opportunity to redirect the world's evolution towards a more equitable and sustainable future.

Notes

1. David Ricardo, *On the Principles of Political Economy, and Taxation* (London: John Murray, 1817) as reprinted in Piero Sraffa (ed.) with the Collaboration of M.H. Dobb, *The Works and Correspondence of David Ricardo*, vol. I (Cambridge, England: University Press for the Royal Economic Society, 1951) p. 356.
2. W.P. Hogart and I.F. Pearce, *The Incredible Eurodollar* (London: George Allen and Unwin, 1982) pp. 130–1.
3. Jürg Niehans, *The Theory of Money* (Baltimore, MA: Johns Hopkins University Press, 1978) pp. 140–1.
4. Gesell investigated the economic disturbances of Argentina's monetary policy and published the first important results of his investigations in a pamphlet: *Die Reformation im Münzwesen als Brücken zum Sozialen Staat* [The Reformation of Currency as the Bridge to the Social State] in 1891. Gesell summarized all of his ideas on political economy in two separate works: Parts I, II, III, and IV with the title *Die Verwirklichung des Rechtes auf vollen Arbeitsvertrag* (Les Huts Geneveys, Switzerland, 1906), and Part V with the title *Die neue Lehre vom Zins* (Berlin, 1911). The second edition of these two books was published as one volume with the title *Die Natürliche Wirtschaftsordnung* (Berlin, 1916) and was subsequently published in English, Spanish and French. The American edition and the revised English edition are published with the title *The Natural Economic Order* (Free-Economy Publishing Co., San Antonio, TX: 1933, and London: Peter Owen, 1958). See also Silvio Gesell, *Die Anpassung des Geldes und seiner Verwaltung and die Bedürfnisse des modernen Verkehrs* [The Reformation of Currency as the Bridge to the Social State] (Buenos Aires: Herpig & Stoeveken, 1897).
5. John Maynard Keynes, *The General Theory of Employment, Interest and Money* (London: Macmillan, 1936) p. 234.
6. Keynes, *The General Theory of Employment, Interest and Money*, Chapter 22, p. 355.
7. Dieter Suhr, *Capitalism at Its Best: The Equalisation of Money's Marginal Costs and Benefits* (Augsburg, Germany: Universität Augsburg, 1989).
8. Hajo Riese, 'Geldökonomie – Keynes und die Anderen: Kritik der monetären Grundlagen der Orthodoxie' in *Ökonomie und Gesellschaft*,

vol. 1: Die Neoklassik und ihre Herausforderungen (Frankfurt, Germany and New York: Campus Verlag, 1983) pp. 103–60.

9. See Hans R.L. Cohrssen, 'Wara' in *The New Republic*, vol. 71, no. 923 (August 10, 1932) pp. 338–9; Hans R.L. Cohrssen, 'Fragile Money' in *The New Outlook*, vol. 162 (September 1933) pp. 39–41; Hans R.L. Cohrssen, *Das beginnende Engagement der Wissenschaft – Für eine gesunde Geldordnung: Eine historische Besinnung* (Boll, Germany: Seminar für freiheitliche Ordnung, 1983); Arthur Dahlberg, *When Capital Goes on Strike: How to Speed Up Spending* (New York and London: Harper and Brothers, 1938); Irving Fisher, *Booms and Depressions: Some First Principles* (London: George Allen and Unwin, 1933); Hansjörg Herr, 'Geld: Störfaktor oder Systemmerkmal?' in *Prokla*, vol. 16/2 (Juni 1986) pp. 108–31; Hansjörg Herr, 'Ansätze monetärer Währungstheorie: Eine Keynesianische Kritik der orthodoxen Theorie' in *Konjunkturpolitik*, vol. 33/1 (1987) pp. 1–26; Leland B. Yeager, 'Essential Properties of the Medium of Exchange' in *Kyklos*, vol. 21 (1968) pp. 45–69; Leland B. Yeager, 'Stable Money and Free Market Currencies' in *Cato Journal*, vol. 3/1 (Spring 1983) pp. 305–26.

10. Margrit Kennedy, *Interest and Inflation Free Money: How to Create an Exchange Medium that Works for Everybody* (Steyerberg, Germany: Permakultur Institut, 1986).

11. Hazel Henderson, *Politics of the Solar Age* (New York: Doubleday, 1981); Margrit Kennedy, *Interest and Inflation Free Money: How to Create an Exchange Medium that Works for Everybody* (Steyerberg, Germany: Permakultur Institut, 1986); Yoshito Otani, *Ursprung und Lösung des Geldproblems* (Neu Ulm, Germany: Arrow Verlag, 1981); Dieter Suhr, *Capitalism at Its Best: The Equalisation of Money's Marginal Costs and Benefits* (Augsburg, Germany: Universität Augsburg, 1989).

12. Suhr, *Capitalism at its Best*, p. 112.

13. Hugo Godschalk, *Die geldlose Wirtschaft: Vom Tempeltausch bis zum Barter-Club* (Berlin: Basis, 1986); and Friedrich Preisigke, *Girowesen im griechischen Ägypten enthaltend Korngiro, Geldgiro, Girobanknotariat mit Einschluß des Archivwesens* (Strassburg, France: Verlag von Schlesier & Schweikhardt, 1910 reprinted: Hildesheim, New York: Georg Olms, 1971).

14. Cohrssen, 'Fragile Money'.

15. Irving Fisher, Hans R.L. Cohrssen and Herbert Fisher, *Stamp Scrip* (New York: Adelphi & Co., 1933).

16. Paul Elkins, *The Living Economy: A New Economics in the Making* (London and New York: Routledge & Kegan Paul, 1986).

17. Keynes, *The General Theory of Employment, Interest and Money*, p. vi.

18. Hans Langelutke, *Tauschbank und Schwundgeld als Wege zur zinslosen Wirtschaft: Vergleichende Darstellung und Kritik der Zirkulationsreformen P.J. Proudhons und Silvio Gesells* (Jena, Germany: Gustav Fischer, 1925) p. 27; and Suhr, *Capitalism at Its Best*, p. 86.

6 Reforming the International Monetary System Towards a World Central Bank: A Summary of Proposals and Fallacies

Bernhard G. Gunter[1]

I. INTRODUCTION

Fifty years after the Bretton Woods conference there is a considerable desire to reform the international monetary system. The major objections to the present 'non-system' emerge from considerably adverse effects from exchange-rate volatility and capital flow volatility. While exchange-rate volatility affects both industrial and developing countries,[2] mainly developing countries suffer from capital-flow volatility. Under the current non-system of unregulated financial markets, capital flows into those markets where fund managers and investors believe the best returns are possible. These beliefs may or may not be consistent with macroeconomic fundamentals. In any case, whenever these beliefs change, capital flows change also, causing high volatility. The further integration of the world economy promises not only an unprecedented opportunity to achieve greater efficiency and higher economic growth but implies also increased volatility, higher risk and subsequent financial crises. The December 1994 Mexican peso crisis was only the tip of the iceberg. Another 'core weakness of the current international monetary system is that the currencies of a few industrial countries constitute the foreign exchange reserves of others and thus become the means of settlement of payment imbalances'.[3]

Unfortunately, there is considerable disagreement on how and to what extent the international monetary system should be reformed. The reform proposals vary in degree from increased macroeconomic policy coordination to the creation of a World Central Bank. The next section provides an overview of current proposals, though detailed discussions of each proposal are not intended. Interested readers are referred to the other chapters in this volume and the literature in the reference section. Some of the proposals are also reviewed in the collection of articles of the Bretton Woods Commission,[4] the United Nations Conference on Trade and Development (UNCTAD),[5] and in the recently edited books by Bordo and Eichengreen, by Kenen and by Teunissen.[6] Solomon provides a short overview of the reform efforts in the 1960s and looks at some of the proposals for reform of the exchange-rate regime, of the policy coordination process, and of the functions and governance of the International Monetary Fund (IMF).[7] For proposals of institutional reforms within the IMF, which are of similar importance, see the *Rethinking Bretton Woods Conference Report*[8] and other contributions to this Series on Rethinking Bretton Woods.[9]

PROPOSALS FOR EXCHANGE-RATE STABILITY

Increased Coordination of Macroeconomic Policies

One of the first serious attempts to coordinate macroeconomic policies internationally was made at the fourth G–7 Economic Summit in Bonn, Germany, in 1978, when Germany, Japan and the United States agreed to pull the world economy out of the stagnation which followed the 1974 oil shock. Although there was some initial success, the fear of rising inflation and government deficits, especially in Germany, soon led to withdrawals from agreed expansionary policies. In the following years, there was little or no international macroeconomic policy coordination. The G–7 Economic Summits had lost their earlier spirit of policy coordination and degenerated into mammoth media events without concrete results. The proposal of 'increased macroeconomic coordination' has become a meaningless slogan, a proposal everybody can agree to without making any real commitments and without any positive consequences for the stability of the international monetary system.

The often-praised Plaza Accord of the G–5 finance ministers and their central bank governors in September 1985,[10] convinced the exchange-rate markets that the value of the US dollar was too high. Consequently, the US dollar fell, until, two years later, the G–7 agreed in the Louvre Accord that the value of the US dollar had fallen enough. Beyond the agreement to coordinate interventions in international currency markets, there was, however, no actual macroeconomic policy coordination. Coordinated central bank interventions in foreign-exchange markets were successful in influencing exchange rates in the 1980s, but have been insufficient in the 1990s, as the European exchange-rate turbulences of September 1992 and August 1993 – and the 1994 Mexican peso crisis – have shown. Speculators and market forces are now large enough to work even against coordinated exchange-rate interventions of the G–7's central banks.

Although the international coordination of macroeconomic policies has been on the agenda for years, it is doubtful if macroeconomic policies have ever been coordinated successfully in practice for more than a very limited time. National interest has always dominated macroeconomic policies in the past and will continue to dominate these policies in the future if there is no institutional framework which limits the impacts of short-term national interests.

Furthermore, the problem of macroeconomic policy coordination is not only a political one but also a technical one. Even if there were sufficient political will to coordinate macroeconomic policies to some degree, this would neither prevent volatile exchange rates nor volatile capital flows. As long as there are national macroeconomic policies, there will always be disequilibria and surprises; market developments cannot be planned and outcomes are neither uniform nor homogeneous. The technical problem of macroeconomic policy coordination is that there are time lags in recognizing, coordinating and implementing the appropriate policy responses. In the meantime, asset prices will not only adjust but also overshoot and thus destabilize the international monetary system, as Rudiger Dornbusch demonstrated nearly 20 years ago.[11] His explanation for overshooting exchange rates, based on different speeds of price adjustments in goods and asset markets, has become a cornerstone to understanding international finance and open macroeconomics.

Capital Controls

These above instabilities are inherent in a system of national macroeconomic policies and free capital movements. The mobility of capital has been promoted and facilitated by financial liberalizations implemented over the last three decades, which drastically reduced any form of capital controls. Consequently, doubts have emerged as to the appropriateness of financial liberalizations. As the *World Development Report 1995* points out, there are both optimistic and pessimistic views on whether increased capital mobility is a blessing or a curse.[12] Carlos Diaz-Alejandro argued forcefully more than ten years ago that the financial liberalizations carried out in several Latin American countries during the 1970s provoked the financial crises of 1983.[13]

Furthermore, positive experiences from national regulations like the ones undertaken by the US Securities and Exchange Commission (SEC) have led economists like Stephany Griffith-Jones to argue for closer international cooperation in the regulation and supervision of financial institutions and markets,[14] which is necessary in order to safeguard the financial system and to prevent an erosion of prudential standards. An emerging consensus, especially after the Mexican peso crisis, seems to be that gradual financial liberalization is preferred. This does not imply that financial-sector reforms should be avoided but it calls for a selective choice of reform measures. The sequencing of financial-sector reforms has been reviewed recently by Vicente Galbis, who concluded:

> One important principle seemingly valid for all cases is the need to accompany financial sector liberalization with the introduction and/or the enforcement of an adequate degree of prudential regulation and supervision. Otherwise, there is the risk that the efficiency gains from liberalization could be offset, at least partially, by adverse loan selection leading to a financial crisis in the form of unsound portfolios of financial institutions, which in turn could raise real interest rates to excessively high levels.[15]

Some capital controls may actually be necessary to avoid negative side-effects and spill-over effects. Those countries which exerted some kind of capital controls at the time of the December 1994 Mexican peso crisis, for example Chile and Colombia, have been considerably less affected by Mexico's devaluation, the so-called 'Tequila effect', than other Latin American countries. Chile seems to have learned its lessons after its financial crisis of the early 1980s. Against many advocates of further financial liberalizations, Chile insisted on keeping some controls on capital transfers.

A promising development is that even the IMF has reconsidered the possibility of imposing capital controls after many small developing countries experienced negative side-effects from sudden capital inflows.[16] Some countries have already started to re-impose some controls on capital flows. However, the IMF views controls on capital flows as transitory measures. The main reason is that most capital controls themselves have negative side-effects for the efficient allocation of resources. The distortions are even larger for cases of asymmetric liberalizations, whereby some countries impose controls while others liberalize their financial sectors. Another argument against capital controls is that they are often ineffective as the size of capital flight after the 1982 debt crisis has shown. The *World Development Report 1995* correctly points out, 'one indisputable fact is that capital crosses borders more easily than labor and despite the best efforts of national governments to control it'.[17] But many neglect to remember that in the early phases of the European Monetary System (EMS), European countries successfully reconciled divergent national policies with exchange-rate stability by restricting international capital movements.[18]

Instead of imposing capital controls, James Tobin, a prominent monetary economist and winner of the 1981 Nobel Prize for Economics, proposed to tax foreign-exchange transactions more than 20 years ago.[19] The Tobin tax has recently gained some popularity: it is supposed to play the role of the sand in the wheels of international finance without harming trade and long-term adjustments.[20] However, the Tobin tax is still falling in disgrace within the financial world, which fears 'the sand in the wheels' while neglecting the current costs of exchange-rate instability. The transaction costs of volatile flexible exchange rates are a multiple of Tobin's 0.5 per cent tax on currency transactions. Consequently, the negative effects on international trade from exchange-rate instability are a multiple of the negative effects from the Tobin tax. The IMF could easily be a supporter of the Tobin tax, especially since one of its statutory purposes is to promote exchange-rate stability.[21]

The Tobin tax is, however, not the first-best solution. As Tobin himself wrote: it is a realistic second-best option to reduce speculative capital movements and thus the volatility of exchange rates. Moreover, it is a source of potential revenues for governments and international organizations.[22] On the other hand, the tax is – in a manner similar to strengthened IMF surveillance and fuller disclosure – not sufficient to prevent speculation and exchange-rate volatility once a speculative drive against a currency has started. Some economists fear that the Tobin tax may delay necessary adjustments in exchange-rate markets and thus contribute to the creation of speculative bubbles.[23] This fear would make sense if the tax would be high enough to prevent long-run adjustments; the fear is baseless, however, at the suggested level of 0.5 per cent. The optimal level of the Tobin tax could be determined by a cost-benefit analysis. Modifications and alternative options to the Tobin tax are just emerging.[24]

The costs of the Tobin tax and capital controls could be avoided by implementing the first-best solution, a World Central Bank. Until then, the Tobin tax, selective capital controls and a set of supervisory and regulatory responses are necessary to counterbalance the increasing exchange-rate instability and to prevent future financial crises.

Target Zones or Flexible Exchange-Rate Bands

Target zones for the dollar, the yen and the European currencies, similar to the exchange-rate bands of the European Monetary System (EMS) have been proposed for many years, especially by John Williamson, Senior Fellow at the Institute for International Economics. Target zones are supposed to limit the variability of nominal or real exchange rates without fixing exchange rates to a specific value. The proposal has gained support from France[25] and the Bretton Woods Commission.[26] However, IMF Managing Director Michel Camdessus and US Treasury officials still oppose the proposal.[27] Critics of target zones object that governments are not able to determine the correct fundamental equilibrium target zones. Furthermore, when rational economic agents realize that the target zone is unrealistic, speculative attacks will be strong enough to destroy them. Thus, Krugman concluded years ago, target zones tend to stabilize exchange rates toward the middle of the band while they are credible, but are subject to speculative attacks when they are not.[28] A more fundamental problem with the target-zone proposal is that once they have been established, individual countries actually have incentives to abuse them and there is no authority to prevent sovereign states from doing so. Similar to the EMS, target zones may still be a first step,[29] especially if they are combined with increased coordination, surveillance and disclosure policies.

Return to Fixed Exchange Rates

An even stronger proposal for reducing the volatility of exchange rates has been made by Ronald McKinnon.[30] He proposed that the central banks of Germany, Japan and the United States jointly announce fixed nominal exchange-rate targets. The proposal includes the need to coordinate monetary policy in order to achieve a constant price level for traded goods. However, the problem again is that there is no mechanism to ensure that fiscal and monetary discipline is exercised to preserve the announced fixed exchange rate. As long as there is no such mechanism, there is no protection against misalignments and consequent speculative attacks.

Return to Gold Standard

Based on the missing enforcement mechanism and other problems of a fixed exchange-rates system, Judy Shelton argues, in her recent book *Money Meltdown*, for a return to a gold standard to restore order in the global currency system.[31] There is one principal objection against a return to a gold standard. The growth rate of the world money supply would be fixed to the growth rate of gold reserves, instead of to the growth rate of world output. This could imply either inflation or deflation, depending on the demand and supply of gold. The reference to a basket of goods, as suggested in Chapter 5 of this volume, would reduce the possibility of a discrepancy between the growth rate of the resources in the basket and the growth rate of the world economy, but would not eliminate the possibility of a discrepancy. With a growing scarcity of resources, one could expect that based on such a money-supply rule, the world economy could be pushed into a deflationary process, similar to the one of the Great Depression.[32]

A World Central Bank

> Bretton Woods rules cannot be resurrected, primarily because capital mobility has made it very difficult to manage exchange rates with narrow bands and occasional jumps in central rates. But that is no reason for failing to design rules that would be equally appropriate to our age.[33]

The idea of a World Central Bank was originally proposed by

John Maynard Keynes in the early 1940s.[34] Keynes proposed the creation of a new international currency unit, the bancor, which would be issued by an International Clearing Union and which would have a fixed but adjustable price in terms of gold. However, when it was clear that the United States did not support such a far-reaching proposal, Keynes' vision of a World Central Bank was not a substantial part of the conference in Bretton Woods, although it led to the creation of the IMF. In the early 1960s, Triffin extended the Keynes Plan in a series of proposals, including the adoption of a single clearing and reserve center for national central banks and a more deliberate expansion of reserve assets.[35] The following years have shown a rich discussion of Triffin's proposal, but with no concrete results.[36]

By the early 1970s, when the Bretton Woods system was in serious trouble, the proponents of a flexible exchange-rate system dominated the scene. However, the time of euphoria was short. Soon the world realized the inadequacy of this new international monetary system. The 1980s have shown again a rich discussion of the proposal for a World Central Bank. In 1983, Stanley Fischer analyzed several models of the world monetary system, including a World Central Bank and a single world money.[37] He described what it would take for the IMF to become a World Central Bank. In 1984, Richard Cooper proposed a new central monetary authority, similar to a World Central Bank.[38]

The restructuring of the international monetary system was also analyzed in Makhijani and Browne. They proposed a comprehensive system which would include the establishment of a World Central Bank but which would be able to 'avoid the deflation-creating conditionalities and adjustment measures that plague countries experiencing deficits under the current system'.[39] In 1987, Mullineux argued that the international money and banking system needs the creation of a new order, he then analyzed the question of the need for a World Central Bank.[40] The idea of a World Central Bank is also supported by Walter Russel Mead.[41]

Today, 50 years after the conference of Bretton Woods, the *Human Development Report 1994* asserts that a World Central Bank is essential for the twenty-first century. According to the *Human Development Report 1994*, the World Central Bank should perform five functions:

- help stabilize global economic activity,

- act as a lender of last resort to financial institutions,

- calm the financial markets when they become jittery or disorderly,

- regulate financial institutions, particularly the deposit banks, and

- create and regulate new international liquidity.

Several options are possible in establishing a World Central Bank.[43] Richard Cooper has suggested several times that the major manufacturing regions – the European Union, Japan and the United States – should start to establish a single currency.[44] Other nations could join later. Quite a few proposals suggest transforming the IMF into a World Central Bank[45] and extending the usage of SDRs to make them what they were intended to be: the principal reserve asset in the international monetary system.[46] Further proposals, like the creation of a new IMF facility[47] or a new instrument to help countries facing unexpected foreign exchange-rate crises, can be complementary tasks.

The transformation of the IMF into a World Central Bank should include the tasks currently handled by the Bank for International Settlement (BIS), the Basle-based central bankers' bank that was originally established in 1930 to deal with the reparation payments of World War I. Under the present financial arrangements the quickest way of dealing with a financial emergency is through the BIS. The BIS assumes a more global role, especially since the US Federal Reserve Bank (Fed) decided to take up its two seats on the board of the BIS, in July 1994. The Fed's move is generally interpreted as a clear trend by the US government towards greater internationalization of banking activities. The World Central Bank could, like the UN system, have different locations. Basle could be the center for all tasks related to banking regulations.

The call for a World Central Bank is influenced by the creation of the European Monetary Institute in Frankfurt, in November 1994, the forerunner of a European Central Bank, and by the plan of the Maastricht Treaty to create a single European currency. Furthermore, the urge for a World Central Bank is a consequence of: (a) dissatisfaction with the current system, especially after the renewed volatility of the dollar in June 1994, (b) unfulfilled promises to coordinate macroeconomic policies, and (c) unavailability of any other reasonable long-term solution.

FALLACIES OF ARGUMENTS AGAINST A
WORLD CENTRAL BANK

Most of the proposals to reform the international monetary system are no longer applicable to the integrated world economy of the twenty-first century.[48] It is now common knowledge that a small disturbance can provoke a large balance-of-payments crisis and that countries can experience pressures on their currency even if macroeconomic policies and performance are sound, as Griffith-Jones with Papageorgiou pointed out in Chapter 3, referring to the G–10 Dini Report.[49] Exchange-rate volatility and speculative attacks on currencies are global problems which need global solutions. A World Central Bank is such a global solution.

Unfortunately, there remain a number of arguments against a World Central Bank. However, most of these arguments presume a disintegrated world economy, that is, a world economy seen as the summation of economies of nation states. This concept of economically independent nation states is no longer valid. This section summarizes some of the fallacies in arguments against a World Central Bank.

The Fallacy of a Loss in Sovereignty

It is a common fallacy that a World Central Bank implies a loss of national sovereignty. This is, however, not the case, as Richard Cooper has pointed out:

> It is an exercise of sovereignty, not an abrogation of sovereignty, to agree on a common endeavor with other sovereign nations. The key question that should be asked is whether, on balance, the particular exercise of sovereignty leaves the participants better or worse off.[50]

Related to the legal aspect of sovereignty is the economic aspect of monetary autonomy, which implies another fallacy.

The Fallacy of National Monetary Autonomy

Governments and central banks fear the loss over their monetary autonomy but ignore the fact that such autonomy is largely lost already. The basic textbook model, which shows that a system of flexible exchange rates provides monetary autonomy, is largely inaccurate today. The degree of integration into the world economy, even for large countries like the United States, leaves little room for genuine monetary autonomy: 'Clearly, flexible rates have not been the panacea which their more extravagant advocates had hoped.'[51] Uncoordinated monetary policy has future repercussions which are not taken into account either in simple textbook models or by most policymakers.

Furthermore, many economists are still tempted to assign monetary policy a larger role than it can perform. Although long-run neutrality of monetary policy may be doubted, a country's real aggregates are largely determined by real factors, such as differences in real wages and productivity.

The Fallacy of Net Benefits from High Inflation

It is argued that many governments, especially of developing countries, are dependent on revenues from high inflation, the so-called inflation tax, which would be lost with an independent anti-inflationary World Central Bank. However, it is highly questionable whether this kind of revenue is in fact beneficial for a country. First of all, inflation is a highly unfair burden on the poor, since inflation is one of the most regressive of all taxes.[52] Second, there is enough evidence that inflation (as well as deflation) is a barrier to sustainable economic growth. Third, high inflation implies high currency devaluation which is likely to have negative effects on the terms of trade, especially if they are combined with currency devaluations of other developing countries which export basically the same kind of goods.

This does not deny that there are revenues in form of seigniorage. Seigniorage and inflation tax revenues are not the same, even though most of the literature uses the terms as synonyms.[53] The correct definition of seigniorage takes into account relative changes in the money demand relative to the price level, which is also called changes in the real money balances. As inflation rates increase, the demand for real money balances decreases. In other words, revenues in the form of seigniorage reach their maximum at a much lower inflation rate than revenues from the inflation tax because real money balances fall as inflation rates increase. Taking into account all the costs of high inflation the net seigniorage benefits are limited to seigniorage raised from a non-inflationary growth in money supply.

The Fallacy of Small Optimum-Currency Areas

The concept of optimum-currency areas was introduced by Robert Mundell and Ronald McKinnon in the early 1960s.[54] The concept implies a cost-benefit analysis for the adoption of a single currency. The optimum-currency area is defined as the area for which the benefits of a single currency are higher than the costs. The United States is generally considered such an area. The Commission of the European Communities evaluated the benefits and costs of a European monetary union and declared that one market requires one currency.[55] On the other hand, it is generally assumed that the world is too diverse and too poorly integrated to benefit economically from a single currency. That assumption is based on several fallacies. First, diversity is no obstacle to a single currency. The problem is not diversity but inadequate policies to make the world safe for diversity. This implies policies for a more equal income distribution on a national as well as international level. Second, even if it may be true that the world economy is currently still too poorly integrated to benefit economically from a single currency, the argument becomes less and less valid as the world economy moves continuously toward further integration. Finally, most analyses of optimum-currency areas calculate purely economic costs and benefits. A more comprehensive analysis, taking into account social, political and psychological aspects, is missing. It is necessary to argue as Paul Krugman did for a single European currency: 'Economic efficiency is not everything. A unified currency is almost surely a necessary adjunct of ... political unification, and that is a more important goal than the loss of some flexibility in adjustment.'[56]

High Costs of a World Central Bank?

Most people fear that the setting up of a World Central Bank involves huge bureaucratic costs. Moreover, since the poorer countries cannot be asked to pay part of the cost, the creation of a World Central Bank is seen as an act of altruism by the industrial countries. This fallacy has three aspects. First, bureaucratic costs of a World Central Bank are probably not much higher than bureaucratic costs of the International Monetary Fund and certainly less than the sum of costs of all central banks together. Second, the economic costs of the current international monetary system are often neglected.[57] Finally, a World Central Bank, issuing one single world currency, would imply considerable gains from international stability and thus, increased international trade and real economic growth.

Political Arguments Against a World Central Bank

Much opposition against any new international institution stems from two other factors. One is that many international institutions are relatively ineffective because national governments did not provide them with enough authority to rule over short-term nation-state interests. The other factor is that centralized governments often neglect the principle of subsidiarity. The postulate has to be that global problems have to be dealt by international institutions and local problems have to be solved by indigenous institutions.

CONCLUSION – WHERE DO WE STAND?

There is some agreement that the current international monetary system, which is often correctly characterized as a non-system, is not sustainable. As Naim has pointed out, 'Mexico's crisis is as much a story about the new international financial system as it is a story about Mexico.'[58] And Neu has observed 'Both proponents and opponents of formally fixed exchange rates would agree that some international institution, arrangement, or forum for fostering international macroeconomic coordination or cooperation would be useful.'[59] However, the solutions proposed by the G–7 Economic Summit at Halifax, which include little more than improved surveillance of national economic policies and fuller disclosure, are not sufficient. Even the set-up of an emergency financing mechanism will not be a solution since governments and market participants will take its existence into account, and may thus lead to less careful actions in the future, a problem which is well known under the term moral hazard.

A stable international monetary system is a world public good. A single world currency, issued by a World Central Bank, is the first-best solution. Its creation is neither impossible nor is it as improbable as many would think. Most economic arguments against a World Central Bank are based on some fallacies. Political arguments are more difficult to deal with. One important political factor which hinders the establishment of a World Central Bank is that 'the industrial countries are deeply preoccupied with their own economic and social problems'.[60] Thus, there seems little room for fundamental changes in the current situation. Consequently, many economists who are generally supportive of a more fundamental solution, now offer marginal proposals in the hope that they will be more acceptable to the leading industrial countries.[61] These marginal proposals embody the danger that needed long-term radical transformations in the relationship between the North and the South are hushed up in a busy agenda which has to deal with problems partly created by marginal proposals.

On the other hand, there are at least four strong arguments which support the proposal of a World Central Bank. First, the costs of the current non-system are growing over time: 'In the not very distant future nominal exchange rate flexibility among major currencies may create more disturbances for the real productive side of national economies than it corrects.'[62] Second, 'recent developments have stressed the importance of altruistic behavior, of cooperative solutions to problems and the costliness of conflict and unregulated pursuit of self-interest'.[63] Third, there is growing consensus that

> cooperation does not entail a sacrificing of national interests. It does not entail a surrendering of effective national sovereignty. It is not a synonym for altruism or international harmony. . . . The essence of cooperation is merely that the various governments take into account the interaction among their economies and policies, and as a result, mutually adjust their policies *so that each nation can act intelligently to better achieve its own, selfish objectives.*[64]

Fourth, it becomes clear that marginal proposals are not a long-run solution. A credible long-run solution must include a mechanism that ensures that fiscal and monetary discipline is exercised to preserve the stability of the international monetary system.[65]

In summary, a World Central Bank is only one aspect of overcoming the growing North–South polarity. Fundamental changes are necessary in order to prevent another cold war, between those who have and those who do not have. The new development vision of equitable, sustainable and participatory development has to be implemented. A new Bretton Woods conference could be the end of the current non-system and the beginning of a new era: 'Once again, as at Bretton Woods 50 years ago, with sufficient will, nations could work together to build a stable and open monetary system for the benefit of the entire international community.'[66]

> We have perhaps accomplished here in Bretton Woods something more significant than what is embodied in this Final Act. We have shown that a concourse of 44 nations are actually able to work together at a constructive task in amity and unbroken concord. Few believed it possible. If we can continue in a larger task as we have begun in this limited task, there is hope for the world.[67]

Notes

1. The author owes special thanks to the staff at the Center of Concern, for the possibility to work on the Rethinking Bretton Woods Project and the cheerful warm-hearted atmosphere. He is indebted to the participants at the 'Rethinking Bretton Woods Conference', of June 12–17, 1994, in Washington, DC, for valuable insights from their discussions, papers and reports. However, the author is alone responsible for the views and ideas expressed in this chapter.
2. De Grauwe concluded that about 20 per cent of the 5.7 percentage point slowdown in the growth of world trade since 1973 can be explained by exchange-rate variability. Paul De Grauwe, 'Exchange Rate Variability and the Slowdown in the Growth of International Trade' in *International Monetary Fund Staff Papers*, vol. 35 (March 1988) pp. 63–84.
3. Jo Marie Griesgraber (ed.), *Rethinking Bretton Woods Conference Report and Recommendations* (Washington, DC: Center of Concern, 1994) pp. 12–13.
4. Bretton Woods Commission (ed.), *Bretton Woods: Looking to the Future* (Washington, DC: Bretton Woods Commission, 1994).
5. United Nations Conference on Trade and Development (UNCTAD), International Monetary and Financial Issues for the 1990s, Volume IV Special Issue, Proceedings of a Conference sponsored by the Group of Twenty-Four on the Occasion of the Fiftieth Anniversary of the Bretton Woods Conference (New York: United Nations, 1994).
6. Michael D. Bordo and Barry Eichengreen (eds), *A Retrospective on the Bretton Woods System: Lesson for International Monetary Reform*, A National Bureau of Economic Research Project Report (Chicago and

London: University of Chicago Press, 1993); Peter B. Kenen (ed.), *Managing the International Economy: Fifty Years After Bretton Woods*, (Washington, DC: Institute of International Economics, 1994); Jan Joost Teunissen (ed.), *The Pursuit of Reform: Global Finance and Developing Countries* (The Hague: Forum on Debt and Development, FONDAD, 1993).

7. Robert Solomon, 'On the Fiftieth Anniversary of Bretton Woods' in *International Economic Letter*, vol. 14 (August 15, 1994) pp. 1–9. Further reform proposals can be found in Ariel Buira, 'Reflections on the International Monetary System' in *Essays in International Finance*, no. 195 (Princeton, NJ: Princeton University Press, January 1995); Zanny Minton-Beddoes, 'Why the IMF Needs Reform' in *Foreign Affairs*, vol. 74/3 (May/June 1995) pp. 123–33; Catherine Gwin and Richard E. Feinberg (eds), *The International Monetary Fund in a Multipolar World: Pulling Together* (New Brunswick, NJ and Oxford, UK: Transaction Books, 1989); D.W. Jorgenson and J. Waelbroeck, *The International Monetary System and Its Reform*, Papers prepared for the Group of Twenty-Four by a United Nations project directed by Sidney Dell, 1979–1986 (Amsterdam *et al.*: North Holland, 1987); and the articles in the Special Issue on The Evolving International Monetary System, *World Development*, vol. 15, no. 12 (December 1987).

8. Griesgraber, *Rethinking Bretton Woods Conference Report and Recommendations*.

9. Aspects of governance of the IMF are also analyzed in Buria, 'Reflections on the International Monetary System', pp. 29–35.

10. Sceptics note that the dollar had already been falling for six months before the agreement was reached, while others say that the agreement had in effect been put in place by the meeting of the G–5 in Washington in the beginning of the year, see the '*Financial Times* Guide to International Monetary Cooperation', *Financial Times* of April 24, 1995, p. 10.

11. Rudiger Dornbusch, 'Expectations and Exchange Rate Dynamics' in *Journal of Political Economy*, vol. 84/6 (1976) pp. 1161–74.

12. World Bank, *World Development Report 1995: Workers in an Integrating World* (Washington, DC: World Bank, 1995) p. 61.

13. Carlos Diaz-Alejandro, 'Goodbye Financial Repression, Hello Financial Crash' in *Journal of Development Economics*, vol. 19 (Sept.–Oct. 1985) pp. 1–24.

14. See Chapter 3 of this volume.

15. Vicente Galbis, 'Sequencing of Financial Sector Reforms: A Review', IMF Working Paper, WP/94/101, International Monetary Fund, Washington, DC (September 1994) p. 19.

16. *IMF Survey* of May 22, 1995, p. 153 and pp. 163–5. Similarly, the World Bank's Economic Development Institute (EDI) organized a seminar on Capital Flows Volatility on May 30 to June 2, 1995.

17. World Bank, *World Development Report 1995: Workers in an Integrating World*, p. 61.

18. Francesco Giavazzi and Alberto Giovannini, *Limiting Exchange Rate Flexibility: The European Monetary System* (Cambridge, MA: MIT Press, 1989).
19. James Tobin, in his 1972 Janeway Lectures at Princeton, published in 1974, as 'The New Economics One Decade Later', cited in James Tobin, 'A Proposal for International Monetary Reform' in *Eastern Economic Journal*, vol. 4, no. 3-4 (July–October 1978) pp. 153-9; see also Tobin's contribution to the UNDP's *Human Development Report 1994* (New York: Oxford University Press, 1994) p. 70; David Felix, 'Suggestions for International Collaboration to Reduce Destabilizing Effects of International Capital Mobility on the Developing Countries' in United Nations Conference on Trade and Development (UNCTAD), *International Monetary and Financial Issues for the 1990s, Research Papers for the Group of Twenty-Four*, volume III (New York: United Nations, 1993) pp. 47-70; and David Felix, 'The Tobin Tax Proposal: Background, Issues and Prospects' in *Futures*, vol. 27, no. 2 (March 1995), pp. 195-208.
20. See the policy forum on 'Sand in the Wheels of International Finance' in *Economic Journal*, vol. 105 (January 1995) pp. 160-92, with articles by Eichengreen, Tobin and Wyplosz; Garber and Taylor, and Kenen. See also Mahbub Ul Haq, Inge Kaul and Isabelle Grunberg (eds), *The Tobin Tax: Coping with Financial Volatility* (New York and Oxford: Oxford University Press, 1996).
21. Article I (iii) of the Fund's Article of Agreement. See also Griffith-Jones and Hans Singer in *Financial Times* of June 14, 1995, p. 14, who argued that measures to reform and strengthen the IMF's resources and surveillance role are welcome, but action steps should be taken to deal with the volatility of short-term capital flows.
22. A tax of 0.5 per cent is estimated to yield over $1.5 trillion a year.
23. For some further aspects see the floor discussion of Stephany Griffith-Jones' paper, 'Globalization of Financial Markets and Impact on Flows to LDCs: New Challenges for Regulation' in Teunissen, *The Pursuit of Reform*, pp. 107-10.
24. See, for example, Paul Bernd Spahn, 'International Financial Flows and Transactions Taxes: Survey and Options' in *IMF Working Paper*, WP/95/60 (Washington, DC: IMF, June 1995), who suggested 'a two-tier rate structure – consisting of a low-rate transaction tax plus an exchange surcharge'.
25. *The Reuter European Community Report* of July 1, 1994.
26. Bretton Woods Commission, *Bretton Woods: Looking to the Future*, p. A-1.
27. Camdessus, speaking at the Institute for International Economics on June 7, 1994, said that conditions are still not right to move to a global target range system for exchange rates. A few weeks before, Under-secretary Lawrence Summers characterized proposals for a managed monetary system that would limit exchange-rate variability as 'utopian visions': *International Business & Finance Daily*, June 9, 1994.

28. Paul Krugman, 'Policy Problems of a Monetary Union' in Paul De Grauwe and Lucas Papdemos (eds), *The European Monetary System in the 1990s* (New York: Longman, 1990), as reprinted in Paul Krugman (ed), *Currencies and Crises* (Cambridge, MA: MIT Press, 1992) p. 189.

29. See Bergsten and Williamson in the collected papers of the Bretton Woods Commission, *Bretton Woods: Looking to the Future*, especially on p. C–28

30. Ronald I. McKinnon, *An International Standard for Monetary Stabilization* (Institute for International Economics, Washington, DC, 1984) and Ronald I. McKinnon, 'Monetary and Exchange Rate Policies for International Financial Stability: A Proposal' in *Journal of Economic Perspectives*, vol. 2/1 (1988) pp. 83–103.

31. Judy Shelton, *Money Meltdown: Restoring Order to the Global Currency System* (New York: The Free Press, 1994).

32. In Chapter 5 of this volume, Bernard Lietaer suggests to impose a time-related demurrage charge which would prevent the hoarding of such a currency if the charge is high enough. Lietaer claims that this would lead to an increased velocity, which would then result in an increase of output but not to an increase in prices, since prices are fixed to the basket of commodities. The author of this chapter is doubtful that the proposed reference currency combined with a considerable demurrage charge would be accepted as a means of payments.

33. John Williamson in *Financial Times*, July 8, 1994, p. 16.

34. John Maynard Keynes, 'Proposals for an International Clearing Union' in Herbert G. Grubel (ed.), *World Monetary Reform* (Stanford, California: Stanford University Press, 1963) pp. 55–79. See also Meier, *Problems of a World Monetary Order*, pp. 33–8 for more details.

35. Robert Triffin, *Gold and Dollar Crisis* (New Haven, Connecticut: Yale University Press, 1960); Robert Triffin, 'The Evolution of the International Monetary System: Historical Reappraisal and Future Perspectives' in *Princeton Studies in International Finance*, no. 12 (Princeton, NJ: Princeton University Press, 1964).

36. For a review of the proposals of the 1960s, see Robert E. Cumby, 'Special Drawing Rights and Plans for Reform of the International Monetary System: A Survey' in George M. Von Furstenberg (ed.), *International Money and Credit: The Policy Roles* (Washington, DC: International Monetary Fund, 1983) pp. 435–73.

37. Stanley Fischer, 'The SDR and the IMF: Toward a World Central Bank?' in Von Furstenberg, *International Money and Credit: The Policy Roles*, pp. 179–99.

38. Richard N. Cooper, 'A Monetary System for the Future' in *Foreign Affairs*, vol. 63 (1984) pp. 166–84.

39. Arjun Makhijani and Robert S. Browne, 'Restructuring the International Monetary System' in *World Policy Journal*, vol. 3, no. 1 (Winter 1985/86) pp. 77–8.

40. A.W. Mullineux, *International Money and Banking: The Creation of a New Order* (Brighton, UK: Wheatsheaf Books, 1987).

41. Walter Russel Mead, 'American Economic Policy in the Antemillennial Era' in *World Policy Journal*, vol. 6/3 (summer 1989), pp. 385–468.

42. UNDP, *Human Development Report 1994*, p. 84.

43. For some intermediate steps see, for example, Reginald H. Green, 'Reflections on Attainable Trajectories: Reforming Global Economic Institutions' in Jo Marie Griesgraber and Bernhard G. Gunter (eds), *Promoting Development: Effective Global Institutions for the Twenty-first Century* (London and Chicago: Pluto Press, with Center of Concern, 1995), pp. 38–81; and UNDP, *Human Development Report 1994*, pp. 84–5.

44. See, for example, Richard N. Cooper in the Panel Discussion on 'One Money for How Many?' in Peter B. Kenen (ed.), *Understanding Interdependence: The Macroeconomics of the Open Economy* (Princeton, NJ: Princeton University Press, 1995) pp. 84–8.

45. See Aziz Ali Mohammed, 'A Proposal for Transforming the IMF into a World Central Bank', mimeo, (Washington, DC: Washington Center for Policy and Research, 1994).

46. The intention expressed in the Articles of Agreement of the International Monetary Fund, since 1978, to make the special drawing right the principal reserve asset in the international monetary system has never been realized. For further aspects of this point, see Corden, W. Max, 'Is There an Important Role for an International Reserve Asset Such as the SDR?' as reprinted in: Robert E. Baldwin and David J. Richardson (eds), *International Trade and Finance: Readings*, 3rd ed. (Boston, MA: Little Brown, 1986) p. 358.

47. Kenen, 'Reforming the International Monetary System . . .' p. 36.

48. For an excellent collection of articles on the interdependence of today's economies, see Peter B. Kenen (ed.), *Understanding Interdependence: The Macroeconomics of the Open Economy* (Princeton, NJ: Princeton University Press, 1995).

49. Report by the Group of Ten (G–10), *International Capital Movements and Foreign Exchange Markets*, A Report to the Ministers and Governors by the Group of Deputies (Rome: Group of Ten, 1993).

50. Richard N. Cooper, 'What Future for the International Monetary System?' in Yoshio Suzuki, Junichi Miyake and Mitsuaki Okabe (eds), *The Evolution of the International Monetary System: How Can Efficiency and Stability Be Attained?* (Tokyo: University of Tokyo Press, 1990) p. 296.

51. Tobin, 'A Proposal for International Monetary Reform', p. 153.

52. See, for example, Williamson in the comment to Corden, 'Macroeconomic Policy and Growth: Some Lessons of Experience', p. 86. For a more recent overview of the distributive effects of inflation, see Mario I. Blejer and Isabel Guerrero, 'The Distributive Effects of Macroeconomic Policies: A Survey', mimeo (Washington, DC: IMF,

Monetary and Exchange Affairs Department and World Bank, Economic Development Institute, 1995); and Ales Bulir and Anne-Marie Gulde, 'Inflation and Income Distribution: Further Evidence on Empirical Links', mimeo (Washington, DC: International Monetary Fund, Monetary and Exchange Affairs Department, 1995).

53. A clear formal analysis of the difference between seigniorage and inflation tax revenues can be found in Jeffrey Sachs and Felipe B. Larrain, *Macroeconomics in the Global Economy* (Englewood Cliffs, NJ: Prentice Hall, 1993) pp. 339–40.

54. Robert A. Mundell, 'A Theory of Optimum Currency Areas' in *American Economic Review*, vol. 51/4 (September 1961) pp. 657–65; and Ronald I. McKinnon, 'Optimum Currency Areas' in *American Economic Review*, vol. 53/4 (September 1963) pp. 717–25. For a recent summary review with further references, see George S. Tavlas, 'The Theory of Optimum Currency Areas Revisited' in *Finance & Development*, vol. 30/2 (June 1993) pp. 32–5.

55. Commission of the European Communities, 'One Market, One Money: An Evaluation of the Potential Benefits and Costs of Forming an Economic and Monetary Union' in *European Economy*, vol. 44 (October 1990) pp. 63–8.

56. Krugman, 'Policy Problems of a Monetary Union', p. 203. On the other side are economists like Milton Friedman, who argue that political unification must precede monetary unification; Milton Friedman in *National Review*, September 12, 1994, p. 36.

57. John Williamson emphasized four economic costs of the present non-system: (1) exchange-rate volatility, (2) lack of control over the volume of international liquidity, (3) maldistribution of seigniorage that results from reserve creation, and (4) asymmetry in the position of the US dollar, cited in Gerald M. Meier, *Problems of a World Monetary Order*, 2nd ed. (New York: Oxford University Press, 1982) p. 233.

58. Moises Naim, 'Mexico's Larger Story' in *Foreign Policy*, vol. 112 (Summer 1995) p. 114.

59. C. Richard Neu, *A New Bretton Woods: Rethinking International Economic Institutions and Arrangements* (Santa Monica, CA: Rand Summer Institute, 1993) p. 22.

60. Kenen, 'Reforming the International Monetary System . . .', p. 20.

61. For example, see Richard Cooper, 'What Future for the International Monetary System?' in Yoshio Suzuki, Junichi Miyake and Mitsuaki Okabe (eds), *The Evolution of the International Monetary System: How Can Efficiency and Stability Be Attained?* (Tokyo: University of Tokyo Press, 1990) pp. 277–300.

62. Cooper, 'What Future for the International Monetary System?' p. 299.

63. Nancy Folbre and Samuel Bowles in *The Nation*, December 13, 1993, p. 714.

64. Ralph C. Bryant, 'The Evolution of the International Monetary

System: Where Next?' in Yoshio Suzuki, Junichi Miyake and Mitsuaki Okabe (eds), *The Evolution of the International Monetary System: How Can Efficiency and Stability Be Attained?* (Tokyo: University of Tokyo Press, 1990) p. 36 (italics in the original).

65. 'The lesson for today is that pegged exchange rate systems do not work for long no matter how well they are designed. Pegged exchange rates, capital mobility, and policy autonomy just do not mix.' Bordo, 'The Bretton Woods International Monetary System: A Lesson for Today', p. 10.

66. Margaret Garritsen de Vries, 'The IMF Fifty Years Later' in *Finance and Development*, vol. 32 (June 1995) p. 45.

67. In Keynes' speech during the Verbatim Minutes of the Closing Plenary Session, Bretton Woods, NH, July 22, 1944; reprinted in US Department of State, *Proceedings and Documents of the United Nations Monetary and Financial Conference, Bretton Woods, NH, July 1–22, 1944* (Washington, DC: United States Government Printing Office, 1948) p. 1110; also in Donald Moggridge (ed.), *The Collected Writings of John Maynard Keynes; Volume XXVI: Activities 1941–1946, Shaping the Post-War World: Bretton Woods and Reparations*, (London: Macmillan and Cambridge, MA: Cambridge University Press, 1980), p. 103.

Glossary

African, Caribbean and Pacific (ACP) Countries – Countries entitled to tariff concessions and official development assistance under the Lomé Conventions. As of 1992, roughly 65 developing countries received EC foreign aid in the form of capital investment, debt relief, duty reductions, subsidies, or technical assistance. The aid package for 1996–2000 is projected to be about $15 billion.

African Development Bank – An international development finance institution owned by 76 member governments; 51 regional members from Africa and 25 non-regional, mostly industrialized nations. The Bank, which is headquartered in Abidjan, Cote d'Ivoire, was founded as a purely African self-help initiative in 1963 and began with only US$250 million in capital, none of which came from the world's industrialized nations. In 1982, the AfDB accepted developed countries as members.

Agenda 21 – The main strategy document for environmentally responsible development for the twenty-first century prepared at the United Nations Conference on Environment and Development (UNCED) in Rio de Janeiro, in June 1992. The Agenda 21 action plan covers over 100 program areas, including commitments to allocate international aid to protect natural habitat and diversity and to programs with high returns for poverty alleviation and environmental health.

American Depositary Receipt (ADR) – A certificate issued by a bank in the United States for foreign securities placed in its custody and registered with the Securities and Exchange Commission (SEC). ADRs are denominated in dollars and can be traded in the same manner as stocks issued in the United States.

Asian Development Bank – An international development finance institution owned by 52 member governments; 19 industrialized nations in Europe, North America, Asia and the Pacific, and 33 developing nations. The Bank, which is headquartered in Manila, was created in 1966 on the recommendation of the United Nations Economic Commission for Asia and the Far East to accelerate economic development in the developing countries of Asia.

Balance-of-payments deficit/surplus – The balance of payments consists of the current account (flows of goods and services) and the capital account (flows of financial assets). A country is said to have a balance-of-payments deficit when its income (credits from exports, cash inflows, loans, etc.) is less than its payments (debits from imports, cash outflows, debt repayments, etc.). A balance-of-payments surplus occurs when income is greater than payments.

Bank for International Settlement (BIS) – An intergovernmental financial institution originally established in 1930 to assist and co-ordinate the transfer of payments among national central banks. This contrasts with the Board of Governors of the IMF which is comprised of Ministers of Finance. The creation of the IMF constrained the subsequent expansion of the BIS's international monetary role and activities. Main current activities of the bank are to assist central banks in managing and investing their monetary reserves, and to collect and disseminate information on macroeconomic topics and international monetary affairs.

Beggar-thy-neighbor policies – Economic policies by one country to improve its domestic economy, but which have adverse effects on other economies, such as competitive devaluations and tariffs.

Brady Plan – Named after a March 1989 initiative by then US Secretary of Treasury Nicholas Brady who proposed that countries with sound adjustment programs should get access to debt-reduction facilities supported by international financial institutions and official creditors.

Bretton Woods institutions (BWIs) – The institutions founded at the conference of Bretton Woods, New Hampshire, in 1944, that is, the World Bank and the International Monetary Fund (IMF).

Bretton Woods Commission – A private forum led by former monetary authorities of Europe, Japan and the United States. Also called the Volcker Commission after its chair, Paul Volcker, former chair of the US Federal Reserve Board.

Buy-back – See: Repurchase.

Committee of Twenty (C–20) – Also called 'Committee on Reform of the International Monetary System and Related Issues', established by the IMF's Board of Governors in light of the events following August 15, 1971, when President Nixon suspended the convertibility of dollars into gold. The committee consisted of one member appointed by each country or group of countries which appoints or elects an Executive Director of the Fund. The Committee decided to let a new monetary system evolve gradually out of existing arrangements and completed its work in 1974.

Compensatory and Contingency Financing Facility (CCFF) – The provision of IMF resources for either a temporary export shortfall for reasons largely beyond the member's control or a temporary excess in the cost of cereal imports. The borrowing country has to cooperate with the Fund in an effort to find appropriate solutions for any balance-of-payments difficulties. Repurchases have to be made within three to five years.

Concessionality – A description of lending conditions which reduce the burden to the borrower, like a low interest rate. Concessionality should not be confused with conditionality, which is a description of requirements for borrowers to receive loans.

Debt crisis – Extreme difficulties of many developing countries to repay their loans since 1982, caused mainly by drastically increasing interest rates in the hard currency creditor countries and a slowing world economy which led to lower exports.

Debt Reduction Program – Operational guidelines by the World Bank, adopted in 1989, to provide support over three years to developing countries for the reduction of their debt and their debt-servicing payments. The guidelines were accompanied by a $100 million fund, established by the International Development Association, to help severely indebted, low-income countries reduce their commercial debt.

Debt-swap – A sale of a country's outstanding loans at a discount to a third party and converted into the debtor's local currency. In the case of a debt-for-equity swap, the third party is typically a transnational corporation which uses the repayment in local currency for investment in the debtor country.

Debt write-down – A bank's reduction of the book value, that is, what the bank assesses as its genuine worth, of an outstanding loan. The debt write-down does not necessarily reduce the amount the debtor is required to repay.

Deflation – The opposite of inflation, that is, a sustained fall in the general price level. More generally, although incorrectly, deflation is also used as a sustained reduction of the inflation rate, that is, a lower increase in the general price level.

Depreciation/devaluation – A decrease in the value of a currency. If the exchange rate is defined in terms of foreign currency over domestic currency, then a devaluation of the domestic currency implies a decrease of the exchange rate. If the exchange rate is defined in terms of domestic currency over foreign currency, then a devaluation of the domestic currency implies an increase of the exchange rate.

Development (equitable, sustainable and participatory) – A healthy growing economy which (a) distributes the benefits widely, (b) meets the needs of the present generation without compromising the needs of future generations, and (c) provides for human rights and freedoms, effective governance and increasing democratization.

Development Committee – Officially the 'Joint Ministerial Committee of the Boards of Governors of the World Bank and the IMF on the Transfer of Real Resources to Developing Countries'. Established in October 1974, it currently consists of 24 members, generally Ministers of Finance, appointed in turn to successive periods of two years by one of the countries or groups of countries that designates a member of the World Bank's or the IMF's Board of Executive Directors. The Committee advises and reports to the Boards of Governors of the Bank and the IMF.

Dutch disease – The term refers to the shrinkage of the manufacturing sector after a discovery of natural resources, as factors move from the manufacturing sector to the resource depletion sector. The shrinkage of the manufactured sector can be a source of chronic slow growth as the economy can be considered to exhibit backward and forward linkages as they were, for example, stressed by the economist Albert Hirschman.

Economic and Social Council (ECOSOC) – One of the original six major organs of the United Nations. It coordinates the economic and social work of the United Nations and the specialized agencies and institutions. The Council charged with making recommendations and initiatives relating to all economic and social questions.

Effective Exchange Rate – Unfortunately, the term is used in two different ways: (a) as an artificial number which takes into account the value of a currency in relation to all other currencies, calculated as the weighted geometric average of exchange rates, whereby the weighting is based on the relative amount of trade with other countries; or (b) as the true cost of exchanging one currency for another currency, taking into account taxes and premiums for the exchange. In this volume, the term is only used in the first way.

Enhanced Structural Adjustment Facility (ESAF) – Introduced in 1988, ESAF is disbursed by the IMF as a trustee. Objectives, eligibility, terms and basic program features of ESAF parallel those of the Structural Adjustment Facility (SAF). However, the adjustment measures are much stronger than for SAF and a detailed policy framework paper is prepared each year.

Enhanced Toronto Terms – See: Toronto Terms.

European Bank for Reconstruction and Development (EBRD) – Also known as the European Bank, the EBRD is a development bank created in Paris in 1990 by the European Community and other countries around the globe to finance the economic development of the former Soviet Union and Eastern European countries.

Executive Director – The Executive Directors represent the member governments of the World Bank. According to the Articles of Agreement, the five largest shareholders – the United States, Japan, Germany, France, and the United Kingdom – each appoint one Executive Director. The other countries are grouped into 19 constituencies, each represented by an Executive Director who is elected by a country or a group of countries. The same applies to the Executive Directors of the IMF.

Extended Fund Facility (EFF) – A facility of the IMF that aims to overcome structural balance-of-payments deficits. This program generally lasts for three years, although it may be lengthened to four years. The program identifies policies and measures for the first year in detail. Resources are provided in the form of extended arrangements that include performance criteria and drawings in installments. Repurchases are made in 4 to 10 years.

Externality – A positive or negative spill-over effect from consumption or production of one economic agent to another one, based on the nonexistence of markets, for example, for clean air. It is impossible to define and enforce property rights.

Foreign direct investment – Investment abroad, usually by transnational corporations, involving an element of control by the investor over the corporation in which the investment is made.

Foreign portfolio investment – Investment abroad, mainly in financial (including monetary) assets, whereby the investment is too small to give an investor partial or total control of a company. The sale of these assets allows the investor to back out within a short period of time.

G–5 – Group of Five; the five countries whose currencies make up the Special Drawing Right basket since 1981 (France, Germany, Japan, the United Kingdom, and the United States). Since 1985 the G–5 Finance Ministers meet regularly to coordinate exchange-rate policies. At the 1986 G–7 Summit Meeting in Tokyo, the heads of state agreed to expand the membership of the G–5 Finance Ministers' meeting to include Canada and Italy.

G–7 – Group of Seven; the seven major industrial countries (Canada, France, Italy, Germany, Japan, the United Kingdom, and the United States). Since 1976, G–7 heads of government meet annually at economic summits to coordinate macroeconomic policies. Since 1987, G–7 summits have become mammoth media events, the earlier spirit of informal discussion has been lost, and the serious economic policy making has shifted to the G–7 Finance Ministers' meeting, which may or may not coincide with the G–7 summits. Most recently, Russia also participates at the G–7 summits, although on an as yet undefined basis.

G–10 – Group of Ten; the IMF's ten principal creditor nations (Belgium, Canada, France, Germany, Italy, Japan, the Netherlands, Sweden, the United Kingdom and the United States), created in 1962 to lend money to the IMF, through the so-called General Arrangements to Borrow (GAB). Switzerland, although an initial country creating the GAB, was not considered a member of the G–10, until it became a full member of the IMF in 1992. Until 1983, only the G–10 plus Switzerland could borrow under the GAB. The G–10 is sometimes confused with the Paris Club (see Paris Club). Saudi Arabia is an associate member of the G–10.

G–24 – Group of 24; formed at the 1972 Lima meeting to represent the interests of the developing countries in negotiations on international monetary affairs. The Group's members are: Algeria, Argentina, Brazil, Columbia, Cote d'Ivoire, Egypt, Ethiopia, Gabon, Ghana, Guatemala, India, Iran, Lebanon, Mexico, Nigeria, Pakistan, Peru, the Philippines, Sri Lanka, Syria, Trinidad and Tobago, Venezuela and Zaire. China attends as an invitee.

General Agreement on Tariffs and Trade (GATT) – An agreement signed at the 1947 Geneva Conference on multilateral trade. It set out rules of conduct, provided a forum for multilateral negotiations regarding the solution of trade problems and aimed to eliminate tariffs and other barriers to trade. With the completion of the multilateral trade agreements of the Uruguay Round in 1994, the GATT became the World Trade Organization (WTO). (See also Uruguay Round and World Trade Organization.)

General Resources Account (GRA) – The official term for the account of the general funds available for IMF member countries with balance-of-payments problems.

Generalized System of Preferences (GSP) – Introduced in 1971, the system provides preferential access to the markets of industrial countries for some exports from developing countries.

Global Depositary Receipt (GDR) – Similar to American Depositary Receipts (ADRs), GDRs are certificates issued by a bank outside the United States for foreign securities placed in its custody. GDRs are traded around the world.

Global Environment Facility (GEF) – An entity that provides grants and concessional funds to developing countries for projects and activities that aim to protect the environment. The GEF Secretariat is functionally independent but administratively supported by the World Bank. The UNDP is responsible for technical assistance activities and UNEP provides the secretariat for the Scientific and Technical Advisory Panel, made up of 15 international environmental experts, which advises on environmental issues and solutions to them.

Gold standard – A system of monetary organization under which the value of a country's money is legally defined as a fixed quantity of gold.

Good governance – Governance which (a) separates clearly between what is public and what is private, (b) implies accountability, (c) is based on the rule of law and (d) implies transparent information and decision making.

Great Depression – The most severe economic contraction in recorded history of the world economy. In the United States, for example, real GDP had fallen by 30 per cent and unemployment had increased to over 25 per cent of the labor force in the four years following the stock market crash of 1929.

Grameen Bank – Established by Muhammad Yunus, a former university economics professor, as a nonprofit development action and research project and formally incorporated under a government charter of Bangladesh in 1983, the Grameen Bank provides credit without collateral for the poor rural landless laborers, especially women.

Gross domestic product (GDP) – GDP is the value of all final goods and services produced in the country within a given period.

Gross national product (GNP) – GNP is the value of all final goods and services produced by domestically owned factors of production, whether inside or outside the national borders, within a given period.

Human capital – Investments in people (human resources) to improve their productivity, especially education and job training.

Human development index (HDI) – UNDP's composite measure of human development containing indicators representing three equally weighted dimensions of human development: life expectancy at birth, adult literacy and mean years of schooling, and income per capita in purchasing power parity dollars.

Import substitution policy – A policy of replacing imports with domestic products, which involves charging higher import duties and/or restricting imports through quotas or outright bans.

Inspection Panel – The Inspection Panel is an independent forum established by the Executive Directors of the World Bank and the International Development Association (IDA) in 1993. The purpose of the forum is to provide directly and adversely affected people of a bank-financed project with a forum which investigates if the bank acted in accordance with its own policies and procedures.

Inter-American Development Bank – An international financial institution created in 1959 to help accelerate the economic and social development of its member countries in Latin America and the Caribbean. The Bank is owned by its 46 member countries; 28 regional members from the Western Hemisphere, and 18 non-regional members from Europe, Asia and the Middle East. The Bank's headquarters are in Washington, DC.

International Bank for Reconstruction and Development (IBRD) – Commonly referred to as the World Bank, founded in 1944 at Bretton Woods. A lending institution whose official aim is to promote long-term economic growth that reduces poverty in developing countries (see also: World Bank Group).

International Debt (Discount) Facility (IDF/IDDF) – A proposed but not realized international organization which would deal exclusively with the solution of the debt crisis, as proposed by economists like Peter B. Kenen.

International Development Association (IDA) – An institution within the World Bank Group, established in 1960 to promote economic development in the world's poorest countries.

International Finance Corporation (IFC) – The World Bank Group's investment bank for developing countries, established in

1956. It lends directly to private companies and makes equity investments in them, without guarantees from governments.

International Labour Organisation (ILO) – Established in 1919 by the Treaty of Versailles, the ILO became a specialized agency of the United Nations in 1946. The ILO promotes international cooperation regarding policies designed to achieve full employment, improve working conditions, extend social security and raise general living standards.

International Monetary Fund (IMF) – Established in December 1945 following ratification of the Articles of Agreement of the Fund, formulated at the Bretton Woods conference in 1944. The Fund became a specialized agency of the United Nations in 1947 and acts as a monitor of the world's currencies by helping to maintain an orderly system of payments between all countries. To this end, it lends money to its members facing serious balance-of-payments deficits, subject to a variety of conditions.

International Organization of Securities Commissions (IOSCO) – The international equivalent to the Securities and Exchange Commission (SEC) of the United States. The IOSCO is based in London and holds annual conferences to discuss international regulatory issues on securities.

International Trade Organization (ITO) – In 1947, the United Nations Economic and Social Council (ECOSOC) convened an International Conference on Trade and Development in Havana, Cuba, which drew up the Havana Charter, proposing the establishment of an International Trade Organization under the aegis of the United Nations. The ITO had been part of the original plan for the 1944 Bretton Woods conference. Although 50 countries signed the Havana Charter, it failed to receive the necessary number of ratifications and the idea of a permanent UN trade body was never realized. (See also GATT, UNCTAD and WTO).

Jamaica Agreement – The agreement of the IMF member countries concluded at Kingston, Jamaica, in May 1976, which acknowledged the system of floating exchange rates, reduced the role of gold in the international monetary system, revised the valuation and possible uses of the SDR, and authorized the sale of the Fund's gold reserves for the benefit of developing countries.

Keynes Plan – Proposals of the UK treasury at the Bretton Woods conference in 1944, to establish an International Clearing Union which would function much like a World Central Bank. As John Maynard Keynes (1883–1946) was primarily responsible for their formulation, these proposals were collectively referred to as the Keynes Plan.

Keynesian Revolution – A term used to describe the fundamental change in macroeconomic theory based on John Maynard Keynes' *General Theory of Employment, Interest, and Money* (1936), noted for its concern with aggregate demand and its income-generating effect, the possibility of an equilibrium with unemployment, which discredited both the classical and neoclassical dogma of *laissez-faire*.

Lender of last resort – A country's ultimate lender, especially when it provides credit or guarantees to its national banking system. In the United States, the Federal Reserve System, acting principally through the regional Federal Reserve Banks, is the lender of last resort.

Lomé Convention – A trade and economic cooperation convention signed first in 1975 at Lomé, the capital of Togo, by the European Community (EC) member countries and 46 African, Caribbean and Pacific (ACP) developing countries. The most recent Lomé Convention between the EC and ACP countries was concluded in 1989 and expires in 1999.

London Club – Ad hoc meetings of commercial bankers to restructure loans owed by governments and private entities in countries experiencing payment difficulties. London Club-member commercial banks often require that sovereign debtors have an IMF arrangement and a Paris Club (see below) rescheduling in place.

Marshall Plan – Named after US Secretary of State, General George G. Marshall, the plan provided aid by the United States and Canada to Western European countries to restore their economy after World War II; also known as European Recovery Program.

Mixed economy – A system which combines competitive private enterprise with some degree of government activity. While the allocation of resources is dominated by individual actions through the price mechanism, the government plays some role in determining the level of aggregate demand by means of fiscal and monetary policy.

Monetarism – A school of economic thought which argues that monetary factors like changes in the money supply are the principal cause of the instability in the economy. In particular, monetarists believe that an increase in the supply of money will generate inflation rather than employment.

Money center bank – A bank located in a major financial center that offers national and international banking services. Money center banks provide depository, foreign-exhange and trust facilities.

Most Favored Nation Status – The result of the GATT (or any other trade agreement) whereby all contracting parties guarantee to grant each other the same favorable treatments they offer to any other country. Exceptions are customs unions and free-trade agreements.

Multilateral Investment Guarantee Agency (MIGA) – A member of the World Bank Group, the MIGA helps to smooth the flow of foreign investment by insuring investors against non-commercial risks and providing investment advice and promotion services.

Neoclassical economics – A body of economic theory which uses the general techniques of the original nineteenth-century marginalist economists. Today, it is often combined with the liberal doctrine, which advocates the greatest possible use of markets and the forces of competition within economic activity. Thus, economic policy based on neoclassical economics is often said to use either the neoclassical or the neoliberal paradigm.

Neoclassical synthesis – The synthesis of neoclassical and Keynesian economics which was developed almost immediately after the publication of Keynes' *General Theory of Employment, Interest, and Money* (1936) in an effort to rescue classical and neoclassical theory while allowing it to absorb some of Keynes' insights.

Net flow of capital – The difference between total flow of capital into and out of a country or institution: the net flow of capital is the gross flow of capital out minus the gross flow of capital in. For example, if the total amount of capital which flows into a country exceeds the total amount of capital which flows out of a country, the country is said to be a net creditor country. Thus the net flow of capital is positive.

Official Development Assistance (ODA) – Concessional financial aid to developing countries and multilateral institutions provided by official agencies, including state and local governments. It contains a grant element of at least 25 per cent.

Organization for Economic Cooperation and Development (OECD) – Originally set up as the Organization for European Economic Cooperation (OEEC) to coordinate Marshall Plan aid in 1948, the OECD took on its present form in 1961 in order to encourage economic growth and maintain financial stability among its 24 member countries: Australia, Austria, Belgium, Canada, Denmark, Finland, France, Germany, Greece, Iceland, Ireland, Italy, Japan, Luxembourg, the Netherlands, New Zealand, Norway, Portugal, Spain, Sweden, Switzerland, Turkey, the United Kingdom and the United States. Mexico joined in 1994.

Organization of Petroleum Exporting Countries (OPEC) – Formed in 1960, the organization promotes its member countries' joint national interests, primarily preventing reductions in oil prices, usually by restricting production. It consists of the 13 major oil-exporting countries in the Middle East, Far East, Africa and South America.

Oxfam – A global network of organizations, founded in Oxford, England, that funds self-help projects in developing countries.

Participatory development – Development which includes a mechanism for enabling affected people to share in development projects or programs, beginning with identification all the way through to implementation and evaluation. On the national scale it implies a political system of human rights and freedoms, effective governance and increasing democratization.

Paris Club – Ad hoc meetings of creditor governments since 1956 to arrange renegotiation of debt owed or guaranteed by official debtors to official creditors (see also London Club and G–10).

Policy framework paper – A document which is developed by the IMF in connection with its lending facilities. The policy framework paper contains the information on economic policies and economic projections for the country which uses the facility.

Purchasing power parity (PPP) – A concept which implies in its absolute version that commodities have the same price world-wide when measured in the same currency. The lack of empirical support for the absolute version led to the development of a relative version. The relative version of PPP implies that if prices are rising faster in the domestic economy than in another foreign economy, the domestic currency will go down in value compared to the currency of the foreign economy.

Repurchase (or buy-back) – If a country is unable to pay its debt, the creditor bank may consider selling the debt title to a third party on the secondary market for cash. The debtor country may then consider repurchasing the debt title from the third party. The advantage for the creditor bank is to get some immediate cash; the advantage for the debtor country is that it does not have to repay the full debt. The necessary condition for a repurchase, however, is that the debtor country is considered insolvent at the time the creditor bank sells the debt title.

Sectoral Adjustment Loans (SECALs) – Introduced in 1980, the World Bank's provision of resources within a Structural Adjustment Program (SAP) for loans which target policy reforms at the sectoral level; see also Structural Adjustment Loan (SAL) and Structural Adjustment Program (SAP).

Securities and Exchange Commission (SEC) – An independent agency of the US government set up in 1934 to act as the chief regulator for securities, which includes a wide range of financial assets like equities. There are five commissioners appointed by the US President to terms of five years and a staff of about 1500.

Security Council – The principal policy making body of the United Nations on issues of international security. The Security Council's five permanent members are China, France, Russia, the United Kingdom and the United States. Ten additional members are selected by the General Assembly for rotating two-year terms. The Security Council is the only UN body with enforcement powers, which derive from its ability to organize armed forces and dispatch troops to troubled regions around the world.

Seigniorage – The net revenue obtained by any money-issuing body, generally the country's central bank, that is, the face value of coins or paper money issued minus the costs of coining or printing money. Since the Special Drawing Right (SDR) created by the IMF is partly used as money by the IMF's members, the IMF generates seigniorage similar to any central bank.

Special drawing right (SDR) – The IMF's standard unit of account, introduced in 1969, which IMF member countries may use to settle international trade balances and debts if the member country meets a variety of conditions. The value of one SDR was originally expressed in terms of gold at 1/35 ounce of gold, the par value of the US dollar in 1969. In 1974, the SDR was converted to a value represented by 16 national currencies. Since 1981, the SDR is valued in a basket of the G–5 currencies.

Special Program of Assistance (SPA) – A financial support program for 27 low-income, debt-distressed Sub-Saharan African countries (Benin, Burkina Faso, Burundi, the Central African Republic, Chad, the Comoros, Equatorial Guinea, Ethiopia, The Gambia, Ghana, Guinea, Guinea-Bissau, Kenya, Madagascar, Malawi, Mali, Mauritania, Mozambique, Niger, Rwanda, São Tomé and Principe, Senegal, Sierra Leone, Tanzania, Togo, Uganda and Zambia) that are implementing reform programs in conjunction with the International Development Association (IDA) and the IMF. The countries are (a) eligible for IDA loans, (b) have a projected debt-service ratio of 30 per cent or more, (c) are implementing a policy reform program that is endorsed by the Bank and (d) have reached agreement on a policy framework paper with the IMF. For the third phase of the SPA, known as SPA-3, the participating donors (Belgium, Canada, Denmark, Finland, France, Germany, Italy, Japan, Kuwait, the Netherlands, Norway, Sweden, Switzerland, the United Kingdom, the United States, the African Development Bank and the European Community) provide quick-disbursing balance-of-payments support of $8 billion over the three-year period 1994–96.

Stand-by arrangement – A facility of the IMF permitting members to draw down emergency funds for balance-of-payments crises. The draw-downs are available in addition to other IMF lending facilities.

Structural Adjustment Facility (SAF) – Introduced in 1986, the IMF's provision of resources on concessional terms (0.5 per cent interest per year and repayments within five to ten years) to low-income developing countries facing balance-of-payments problems, conditional on a medium-term structural adjustment program, set out in a policy framework paper (PFP). (See also: Enhanced Structural Adjustment Facility (ESAF) and Extended Fund Facility (EFF).)

Structural Adjustment Loan (SAL) – Introduced in the early 1980s, the World Bank's provision of general budget support to facilitate implementation of policies set out in a structural adjustment program (SAP).

Structural Adjustment Program (SAP) – Long-term assistance from the World Bank and other IFIs which is designed to restore equilibrium and promote economic growth. The original rationale for SAPs was that sound projects were not possible in an unsound policy environment. Thus, SAPs became a new instrument to influence macroeconomic policies of developing countries, based on neoclassical economics, advocating *laissez-faire* and free trade.

Surveillance – IMF members are obligated to provide the IMF with the information necessary for the IMF to monitor and evaluate the country's macroeconomic performance. The concept was adopted in 1977, and modified in 1987 and 1988, and recently strengthened in April 1995, as an aftermath of the Mexican peso crisis.

Sustainable development – Development which meets the needs of the present generation without compromising the needs of future generations.

Terms of trade – The quotient between an index of export prices and an index of import prices. When a country's terms of trade decline, as is the case for many developing countries, it is necessary to export more in order to import the same quantity of goods and services.

Tobin tax – A proposal put forward first in 1972 by US Nobel Laureate James Tobin to tax international currency transactions. Tobin has repeated his proposal many times since then. In his proposal in UNDP's *Human Development Report 1994*, Tobin suggests imposing a tax of 0.5 per cent on foreign-exchange transactions.

Toronto Terms – A menu of options for reducing official debt in low-income, debt-distressed countries. The terms, agreed upon in September 1988 (following an agreement in principle at the economic summit held in Toronto three months earlier), include reduced interest, very long grace and repayment periods and partial write-offs of debt-service obligations during the consolidation period. The terms were enhanced by the Paris Club in 1991 (thus, Enhanced Toronto Terms), providing also a consolidation option at market rates, with a repayment period of 25 years, including a 14-year grace period.

Transnational corporation (TNC) – A large enterprise having a home base in one country but operating wholly or partially owned subsidiaries in other countries. Such corporations expand on an international scale to take advantage of economies of scale and to benefit from enjoying near monopoly status, which power is often used against the interest of the developing countries they operate in.

Trinidad Terms – Proposed by John Major, then the UK Chancellor of the Exchequer, at the Commonwealth Finance Ministers' September 1990 conference in Trinidad and Tobago. These terms would have reduced the stock of outstanding debt owed to Paris Club creditors by two-thirds. However, the Trinidad Terms were not accepted by the creditors, who only adopted the Enhanced Toronto Terms in 1991 (see Toronto Terms).

United Nations Conference on Trade and Development (UNCTAD) – The conference, first convened in 1964, is now a permanent organ of the UN General Assembly. All members of the United Nations or of its specialized agencies are members of the conference which has a permanent executive organ and a permanent secretariat. Its role has been to protect and champion the case of developing countries against the trade policies of the developed countries. UNCTAD's major success has been in promoting the Generalized System of Preferences (GSP).

United Nations Development Programme (UNDP) – Created in 1966, it combined the UN Expanded Programme of Technical Assistance and the UN Special Fund. It is responsible for administering and coordinating development projects and technical assistance provided under the auspices of or in liaison with the UN system of development agencies and organizations.

Uruguay Round – The eighth round of GATT negotiations, launched in September 1986 in Punta del Este (Uruguay) and concluded on April 15, 1994 at Marrakesh (Morocco). It dealt with unfinished business from earlier GATT rounds and new issues, such as trade in services, the protection of intellectual property rights, trade-related investment measures, and especially the establishment of the World Trade Organization (WTO).

White Plan – Proposals of the United States for an International Stabilization Fund, proposed at the Bretton Woods conference in 1944, commonly called the White Plan after its chief author, Harry D. White, Under Secretary of the US Treasury. Unlike the Keynes Plan, the White Plan did not provide for the establishment of a new international means of payment or the extension of credit facilities.

World Bank – See: International Bank for Reconstruction and Development.

World Bank Group – Consists of the International Bank for Reconstruction and Development (IBRD) (commonly referred to as the World Bank), the International Finance Corporation (IFC), the International Development Association (IDA), the International Center for Settlements of Investment Disputes (ICSID), and the Multilateral Investment Guarantee Agency (MIGA), all of them based in Washington, DC.

World Trade Organization (WTO) – The WTO is the successor of the GATT, after a transition period, during which all the major trading nations agree to accept the WTO. It is a procedural umbrella agreement to provide an institutional and organizational framework for the administration of the multilateral trade agreements concluded at the Uruguay Round. (See also General Agreement on Tariffs and Trade, and Uruguay Round.)

Bibliography

Askari, Hossein *The Foreign Debt: National Development Conflict* (New York: Quorum Books, 1986).

Askari, Hossein *Third World Debt and Financial Innovations: The Experiences of Chile and Mexico* (Paris: Organization for Economic Cooperation and Development (OECD), 1991).

Balassa, Bela 'The Purchasing Power Parity Doctrine: A Reappraisal' in *Journal of Political Economy*, vol. 72/6 (December 1964) pp. 584–96.

Baldwin, Robert E. and David J. Richardson (eds) *International Trade and Finance: Readings*, 3rd edn (Boston, MA: Little Brown, 1986).

Bank for International Settlement (BIS) *62nd Annual Report* (Basle: BIS, June 15, 1992).

Black, Stanley W. 'Exchange Rate Policy for Less Developed Countries in a World of Floating Rates' in *Essays in International Finance*, no. 119 (Princeton, NJ: Princeton University Press, 1976).

Blejer, Mario I. and Isabel Guerrero 'The Distributive Effects of Macroeconomic Policies: A Survey', mimeo (Washington, DC: IMF and World Bank, 1995).

Bordo, Michael D. 'The Bretton Woods International Monetary System: A Lesson for Today' in *NBER Reporter* (Winter 1992/93) pp. 7–10.

Bordo, Michael D. 'Is There a Good Case for a New Bretton Woods International Monetary System?' in *American Economic Review*, vol. 85/2 (May 1995) pp. 317–22.

Bordo, Michael D. and Barry Eichengreen (eds) *A Retrospective on the Bretton Woods System: Lesson for International Monetary Reform*, A National Bureau of Economic Research Project Report (Chicago and London: University of Chicago Press, 1993).

Branson, William H. 'The Limits of Monetary Coordination as Exchange Rate Policy' in *Brookings Papers on Economic Activity*, vol. 1986/1, pp. 175–94.

Branson, William and Louka Katseli-Papaefstratiou 'Exchange Rate Policy for Developing Countries' in Sven Grassman and Erik Lundberg (eds) *The World Economic Order: Past and Prospects* (London: Macmillan, 1981) pp. 391–419.

Bretton Woods Commission (ed.) *Bretton Woods: Looking to the Future* (Washington, DC: Bretton Woods Commission, 1994).

Breuer, Richard 'Financial Integration: The End of Geography', paper prepared for the International Organization of Securities Commissions (IOSCO) XVII Annual Conference, London, October 1992.

Bryant, Ralph C. 'The Evolution of the International Monetary System: Where Next?' in Yoshio Suzuki, Junichi Miyake and Mitsuaki Okabe (eds) *The Evolution of the International Monetary System: How Can Efficiency and Stability Be Attained?* (Tokyo: University of Tokyo Press, 1990) pp. 15–38.

Buira, Ariel 'Reflections on the International Monetary System' in *Essays in International Finance*, no. 195 (Princeton, NJ: Princeton University Press, January 1995).

Bulir, Ales and Anne-Marie Gulde 'Inflation and Income Distribution: Further Evidence on Empirical Links', mimeo Washington, DC: International Monetary Fund, Monetary and Exchange Affairs Department, 1995).

Cohen, Benjamin J. *Organizing the World's Money: The Political Economy of International Monetary Relations* (London: Macmillan, 1977).

Cohrssen, Hans R.L. *Das beginnende Engagement der Wissenschaft – Für eine gesunde Geldordnung: Eine historische Besinnung* (Boll, Germany: Seminar für freiheitliche Ordnung, 1983).

Cohrssen, Hans R.L. 'Wara' in *The New Republic*, vol. 71, no. 923 (August 10, 1932) pp. 338–9.

Cohrssen, Hans R.L. 'Fragile Money' in *The New Outlook*, vol. 162 (September 1933) pp. 39–41.

Collins, Patrick *Currency Convertibility: The Return to Sound Money* (London: Macmillan Press, 1985).

Commission of the European Communities 'One Market, One Money: An Evaluation of the Potential Benefits and Costs of Forming an Economic and Monetary Union' in *European Economy*, vol. 44 (October 1990) pp. 63–8.

Committee on the Reform of the International Monetary System and Related Issues (Committee of Twenty) *International Mon-*

etary Reform: Documents of the Committee of Twenty (Washington, DC: International Monetary Fund, 1974).

Cooper, Richard N. *Economic Stabilization and Debt in Developing Countries* (Cambridge, MA: MIT Press, 1992).

Cooper, Richard N. 'Is There a Need for Reform?' in Federal Reserve Bank of Boston (ed.) *The International Monetary System: Forty Years After Bretton Woods*, Conference Series no. 28 (Boston, MA: Federal Reserve Bank, 1984) pp. 19–39; reprinted in Robert E. Baldwin and David J. Richardson (eds) *International Trade and Finance: Readings*, 3rd edn (Boston, MA: Little Brown, 1986) pp. 337–55.

Cooper, Richard N. 'What Future for the International Monetary System?' in Yoshio Suzuki, Junichi Miyake and Mitsuaki Okabe (eds) *The Evolution of the International Monetary System: How Can Efficiency and Stability Be Attained?* (Tokyo: University of Tokyo Press, 1990) pp. 277–300.

Corden, W. Max 'Is There an Important Role for an International Reserve Asset Such as the SDR?' in George M. Von Furstenberg (ed.) *International Money and Credit: The Policy Roles* (Washington, DC: International Monetary Fund, 1993) pp. 213–47; reprinted in Robert E. Baldwin and David J. Richardson (eds) *International Trade and Finance: Readings*, 3rd edn (Boston, MA: Little Brown, 1986) pp. 358–81.

Corden, W. Max 'Exchange Rate Policy in Developing Countries' in *Policy, Research, and External Affairs Working Papers*, WPS 412 (Washington, DC: World Bank, 1990).

Corden, W. Max 'Macroeconomic Policy and Growth: Some Lessons of Experience' in *Proceedings of the World Bank; Annual Conference on Development Economics 1990* (Washington, DC: World Bank, 1991) pp. 59–84.

Dahlberg, Arthur *When Capital Goes on Strike: How to Speed Up Spending* (New York and London: Harper and Brothers, 1938).

Dale, Richard *International Banking Deregulation: The Great Banking Experiment* (Oxford, England: Blackwell, 1992).

Davidson, Paul 'A Modest Set of Proposals for Resolving the International Debt Problem' in *Journal of Post-Keynesian Economics*, vol. 10/2 (Winter 1987/88) pp. 323–38.

Davis, E. Philip 'The Structure, Regulation and Performance of Pension Funds in Nine Industrial Countries', mimeo (Bank of England, 1992).

De Grauwe, Paul 'Exchange Rate Variability and the Slowdown in the Growth of International Trade' in *International Monetary Fund Staff Papers*, vol. 35 (March 1988) pp. 63–84.

Diaz-Alejandro, Carlos 'Goodbye Financial Repression, Hello Financial Crash' in *Journal of Development Economics*, vol. 19 (Sept.–Oct. 1985) pp. 1–24.

Dillard, Dudley 'Silvio Gesell's Monetary Theory of Social Reform' in *American Economic Review*, vol. 32 (1942) pp. 348–52.

Dooley, Michael P. 'Buy-Backs and the Market Valuation of External Debt' in *IMF Staff Papers*, vol. 35/2 (June 1988) pp. 215–29.

Dore, M.H.I. and Lorie Tarshis 'The LDC Debt and the Commercial Banks: A Proposed Solution' in *Journal of Post-Keynesian Economics*, vol. 12/3 (Spring 1990) pp. 452–65.

Dornbusch, Rudiger, 'Expectations and Exchange Rate Dynamics' in *Journal of Political Economy*, vol. 84/6 (1976) pp. 1161–74.

Eaton, Jonathan, Mark Gersovitz and Joseph E. Stiglitz 'The Pure Theory of Country Risk' in *European Economic Review*, vol. 30 (June 1986) pp. 481–513.

Edwards, Sebastian 'The International Monetary Fund and the Developing Countries: A Critical Evaluation' in *National Bureau of Economic Research (NBER) Working Paper Series*, no. 2909 (Cambridge, MA: NBER, 1989).

Eichengreen, Barry, Marcus Miller and Richard Portes (eds) *Blueprints for Exchange Rate Management* (London: Centre of Economic Policy Research, 1994).

Eichengreen, Barry, James Tobin and Charles Wyplosz 'Two Cases for Sand in the Wheels of International Finance' in *Economic Journal*, vol. 105 (January 1995) pp. 162–72.

Elkins, Paul *The Living Economy: A New Economics in the Making* (London and New York: Routledge & Kegan Paul, 1986).

Engels, Wolfram 'Schwundgeld' in *Kapital*, Heft 7 (Juli 1982).

Engels, Wolfram *The Optimal Monetary Unit* (Frankfurt, Germany: Campus, 1981).

Fama, Eugene 'Financial Intermediation and Price Level Control' in *Journal of Monetary Economics*, vol. 12 (July 1983) pp. 7–28.

Felix, David 'Suggestions for International Collaboration to Reduce Destabilizing Effects of International Capital Mobility on the Developing Countries' in United Nations Conference on Trade and Development (UNCTAD) *International Monetary and Financial Issues for the 1990s: Research Papers for the Group of Twenty-Four*, vol. III (New York: United Nations, 1993) pp. 47–70.

Felix, David 'The Tobin Tax Proposal: Background, Issues and Prospects' in *Futures*, vol. 27/2 (March 1995) pp. 195–208.

Finch, David 'The IMF: The Record and the Prospect' in *Prince-*

ton *Essays in International Finance*, no. 175 (Princeton, NJ: Princeton University Press, 1989).

Fischer, Stanley 'The SDR and the IMF: Toward a World Central Bank?' in George M. Von Furstenberg (ed.) *International Money and Credit: The Policy Roles* (Washington, DC: International Monetary Fund, 1993) pp. 179–99.

Fisher, Irving *Booms and Depressions: Some First Principles* (London: George Allen and Unwin, 1933).

Fisher, Irving, Hans R.L. Cohrssen and Herbert Fisher *Stamp Scrip* (New York: Adelphi & Co., 1933).

Frenkel, Jacob 'The International Monetary System: Should It Be Reformed?' in *American Economic Review*, vol. 77/2 (May 1987) pp. 205–11.

Friedman, Milton *A Program for Monetary Stability* (New York: Fordham University Press, 1959).

Friedman, Milton *The Optimum Quantity of Money* (Chicago: Aldine, 1969).

Frydl, Edward J. 'The Challenges of Financial Change' in Federal Reserve Bank of New York, *Annual Report 1985* (New York: Federal Reserve Bank of New York, April 1986) pp. 3–27.

Galbis, Vicente 'Sequencing of Financial Sector Reforms: A Review' in *IMF Working Paper*, WP/94/101 (Washington, DC: International Monetary Fund, September 1994).

Garber, Peter M. 'The Collapse of the Bretton Woods Fixed Exchange Rate System in Michael D. Bordo and Barry Eichengreen (eds) *A Retrospective on the Bretton Woods System: Lesson for International Monetary Reform*, A National Bureau of Economic Research Project Report (Chicago and London: University of Chicago Press, 1993) pp. 461–94.

Garber, Peter and Mark P. Taylor 'Sand in the Wheels of Foreign Exchange Markets: A Sceptical Note' in *Economic Journal*, vol. 105 (January 1995) pp. 173–80.

Garritsen de Vries, Margaret (ed.) *The International Monetary Fund 1972–1978: Cooperation on Trial*, Volume III: Documents (Washington, DC: International Monetary Fund, 1985) pp. 69–97.

Garritsen de Vries, Margaret 'The IMF Fifty Years Later' in *Finance and Development*, vol. 32 (June 1995) pp. 43–5.

Gesell, Silvio *Die Anpassung des Geldes und seiner Verwaltung und die Bedürfnisse des modernen Verkehrs* [The Reformation of Currency as the Bridge to the Social State] (Buenos Aires: Herpig & Stoeveken, 1897).

Gesell, Silvio *Die Verwirklichung des Rechtes auf vollen Arbeitsver-trag* (Les Huts Geneveys, Switzerland, 1906) and Silvio Gesell *Die neue Lehre vom Zins* (Berlin, 1911) both reprinted in Silvio Gesell *Die Natürliche Wirtschaftsordnung*, (Berlin, 1916) and published as an American edition and a revised English edition with the title *The Natural Economic Order* (San Antonio, TX: Free-Economy Publishing Co., 1933; and London: Peter Owen, 1958).

Giavazzi, Francesco and Alberto Giovannini *Limiting Exchange Rate Flexibility: The European Monetary System* (Cambridge, MA: MIT Press, 1989).

Girvan, Norman 'Empowerment for Development: From Condi-tionality to Partnership' in Jo Marie Griesgraber and Bernhard G. Gunter (eds) *Promoting Development: Effective Global Insti-tutions for the Twenty-first Century*, Chapter 2 (London: Pluto Press, 1995) pp. 23–37.

Godschalk, Hugo *Die geldlose Wirtschaft: Vom Tempeltausch bis zum Barter-Club* (Berlin: Basis, 1986).

Gooptu, Sudarshan 'Portfolio Investment Flows to Emerging Markets' in *World Bank Working Paper*, March 1993, WPS 1117 (Washington, DC: World Bank, 1993).

Green, Reginald H. 'Global Economic Institution Reform: Reflec-tions on Attainable Trajectories' in Jo Marie Griesgraber and Bernhard G. Gunter (eds) *Promoting Development: Effective Global Institutions for the Twenty-first Century* (London and East Haven, CT: Pluto Press, with Center of Concern, 1995) pp. 38–81.

Griesgraber, Jo Marie (ed.) *Rethinking Bretton Woods Conference Report and Recommendations* (Washington, DC: Center of Concern, 1994).

Griffith-Jones, Stephany with Vassilis Papageorgiou 'Globalisation of Financial Markets and Impact on Flows to LDCs: New Challenges for Regulation' in Jan Joost Teunissen (ed.) *The Pursuit of Reform: Global Finance and Developing Countries* (The Hague: Forum on Debt and Development, FONDAD, 1993) pp. 65–97, reprinted as Chapter 4 in this volume.

Group of 24 (G–24) *Major Industrial Countries Need Improved Policy Mix*, Press Communiqué on International Monetary Affairs, held on April 25, 1995, as reprinted in *IMF Survey* (May 8, 1995) pp. 141–4.

Group of Ten (G–10) *International Capital Movements and For-eign Exchange Markets*, A Report to the Ministers and Gover-nors by the Group of Deputies (Rome: Group of Ten, 1993).

Guitian, Manuel 'Currency Convertibility: Concepts and Degrees' as reported in *IMF Survey*, vol. 23/8 (April 18, 1994) pp. 113, 116–19.

Grubel, Herbert G. (ed.) *World Monetary Reform* (Stanford, CA: Stanford University Press, 1963).

Gunter, Bernhard G. 'Financial Crises and the Great Depression in Germany, 1927–1933' in *Essays in Economic and Business History*, vol. 13 (1995) pp. 55–70.

Gwin, Catherine and Richard E. Feinberg (eds) *The International Monetary Fund in a Multipolar World: Pulling Together* (New Brunswick, NJ and Oxford, UK: Transaction Books, 1989).

Hahn, Frank M. 'Equilibrium with Transaction Costs' in *Econometrica*, vol. 39/3 (May 1971) pp. 417–38.

Hart, Albert G., Nicholas Kaldor and Jan Tinbergen 'The Case for an International Commodity Reserve Standard' in United Nations Conference on Trade and Development (UNCTAD) *Trade and Development*, vol. VIII: Miscellaneous Documents and List of Participants (New York: United Nations, 1964).

Helleiner, Gerald K., Conrad Blyth, Kenneth Dadzie, William Demas, Stuart Harris, Lal Jayawardena, Jeremy Morse, Harry M. Osha, Indraprasad G. Patel *Towards a New Bretton Woods: Challenges for the World Financial and Trading System*, Report by a Commonwealth Study Group (London: Commonwealth Secretariat, 1983).

Henderson, Hazel *Politics of the Solar Age* (New York: Doubleday, 1981).

Herr, Hansjörg 'Geld: Störfaktor oder Systemmerkmal?' in *Prokla*, vol. 16/2 (Juni 1986) pp. 108–31.

Herr, Hansjörg 'Ansätze monetärer Währungstheorie: Eine Keynesianische Kritik der orthodoxen Theorie' in *Konjunkturpolitik*, vol. 33/1 (1987) pp. 1–26.

Hicks, John 'Monetary Theory and History: An Attempt at Perspective' in John Hicks (ed.) *Critical Essays in Monetary Theory* (Oxford, UK: Clarendon Press, 1967) pp. 1–60.

Hirsch, Fred 'An SDR Standard: Impetus, Elements, and Impediments' in *Essays in International Finance*, no. 99 (Princeton, NJ: Princeton University Press, 1973).

Hogart, W.P. and I.F. Pearce *The Incredible Eurodollar* (London: George Allen and Unwin, 1982).

Howell, Michael and Angela Cozzini *Games without Frontiers: Global Equity Markets in the 1990s* (London: Salomon Brothers, 1991).

International Finance Corporation *Emerging Stock Markets*

Factbook (Washington, DC: International Finance Corporation, various years).

International Monetary Fund (IMF) *World Economic Outlook* (Washington, DC: IMF, various years).

International Monetary Fund (IMF) *International Financial Statistics* (Washington, DC: IMF, various issues).

International Organization of Securities Commissions (IOSCO) *Final Communiqué of the 17th Annual Conference* (London: IOSCO, October 1992).

Jorgenson, D.W. and J. Waelbroeck *The International Monetary System and Its Reform*, papers prepared for the Group of Twenty-Four by a United Nations project directed by Sidney Dell, 1979–1986 (Amsterdam et al.: North Holland, 1987).

Kaldor, Nicholas 'Speculation and Economic Stability' in *Review of Economic Studies*, vol. 7 (October 1939) pp. 1–27; reprinted in Nicholas Kaldor (ed.) *Essays on Economic Stability and Growth* (Glencoe, Illinois: The Free Press of Glencoe, 1960) pp. 17–58.

Kenen, Peter B. 'The Use of IMF Credit' in Catherine Gwin and Richard E. Feinberg (eds) *The International Monetary Fund in a Multipolar World: Pulling Together* (New Brunswick, NJ: Transactions Books, 1989) pp. 69–91.

Kenen, Peter B. 'Organizing Debt Relief: The Need for a New Institution' in *Journal of Economic Perspectives*, vol. 4/1 (Winter 1990) pp. 7–18.

Kenen, Peter B. 'Reforming the International Monetary System: An Agenda for the Developing Countries' in Jan Joost Teunissen (ed.) *The Pursuit of Reform: Global Finance and Developing Countries* (The Hague: Forum on Debt and Development, FONDAD, 1993) pp. 19–41.

Kenen, Peter B. (ed.) *The International Monetary System: Highlights from the Fifty Years of Princeton's Essays in International Finance* (Boulder, CO: Westview Press, 1993).

Kenen, Peter B. (ed.) *Managing the International Economy: Fifty Years After Bretton Woods* (Washington, DC: Institute of International Economics, 1994).

Kenen, Peter B. 'Capital Controls, the EMS and EMU' in *Economic Journal*, vol. 105 (January 1995) pp. 181–92.

Kenen, Peter B. (ed.) *Understanding Interdependence: The Macroeconomics of the Open Economy* (Princeton, NJ: Princeton University Press, 1995).

Kennedy, Margrit *Interest and Inflation Free Money: How to Create an Exchange Medium that Works for Everybody* (Steyerberg, Germany: Permakultur Institut, 1986).

Keynes, John Maynard *The Economic Consequences of the Peace* (London: Macmillan, 1919) reprinted in *The Collected Writings of John Maynard Keynes*, vol. II (London: Macmillan, 1971).

Keynes, John Maynard *The General Theory of Employment, Interest and Money* (London: Macmillan, 1936).

Keynes, John Maynard *Proposals for an International Clearing Union*, British Government Publication, no. 6437 (London: HMSO, 1943) reprinted in Herbert G. Grubel (ed.) *World Monetary Reform, Plans and Issues* (Stanford, CA: Stanford University Press, 1963).

Keynes, John Maynard *The Collected Writings of John Maynard Keynes*, vols. 25 and 26 (Cambridge: Macmillan and Cambridge University Press, 1980).

Kindleberger, Charles P. 'The SDR as International Money' in Paul Coulbois (ed.) *Essais en l'honneur de Jean Marchal*, vol. 2: La Monnaie (Paris, Editions Cujas, 1975) pp. 303–14; reprinted in Charles P. Kindleberger *International Money: A Collection of Essays* (London: George Allen and Unwin, 1981) pp. 63–75.

Kindleberger, Charles, P. 'The Price of Gold and the N–1 Problem' in Charles P. Kindleberger *International Money: A Collection of Essays* (London and Boston, MA: George Allen and Unwin, 1981) pp. 76–86.

Krugman, Paul 'Financing vs Forgiving a Debt Overhang' in *Journal of Development Economics*, vol. 29/3 (November 1988) pp. 253–68.

Krugman, Paul 'Market-Based Debt Reduction Schemes' in Jacob A. Frenkel, Michael P. Dooley and Peter Wickham (eds) *Analytical Issues in Debt* (Washington, DC: International Monetary Fund, 1989) pp. 258–78.

Krugman, Paul 'Policy Problems of a Monetary Union' in Paul De Grauwe and Lucas Papdemos (eds) *The European Monetary System in the 1990s* (New York: Longman, 1990) reprinted in Paul Krugman (ed.) *Currencies and Crises* (Cambridge, MA: MIT Press, 1992) pp. 185–203.

Krugman, Paul and Maurice Obstfeld *International Economics* (3rd ed.) (New York: HarperCollins, 1994).

Langelutke, Hans *Tauschbank und Schwundgeld als Wege zur zinslosen Wirtschaft: Vergleichende Darstellung und Kritik der Zirkulationsreformen P.J. Proudhons und Silvio Gesells* (Jena, Germany: Gustav Fischer, 1925).

Makhijani, Arjun and Robert S. Browne 'Restructuring the International Monetary System' in *World Policy Journal*, vol. 3/1 (Winter 1985/86) pp. 59–80.

Makhijani, Arjun and Robert S. Browne 'The World's Monetary Arrangements: Restructuring the International Monetary System' in *World Policy Journal*, vol. 3/1 (Winter 1985–86) pp. 59–80.

McCallum, Bennett T. 'Two Fallacies Concerning Central-Bank Independence' in *American Economic Review*, vol. 85/2 (May 1995) pp. 207–11.

McCulloch, J. Huston 'Beyond the Historical Gold Standard' in Colin Campbell and W. Dougan (eds) *Alternative Monetary Regimes* (Baltimore, MA: Johns Hopkins University Press, 1986).

McKinnon, Ronald I. 'Optimum Currency Areas' in *American Economic Review*, vol. 53/4 (September 1963) pp. 717–25.

McKinnon, Ronald I. *An International Standard for Monetary Stabilization* (Washington, DC: Institute for International Economics, 1984).

McKinnon, Ronald I. 'Monetary and Exchange Rate Policies for International Financial Stability: A Proposal' in *Journal of Economic Perspectives*, vol. 2/1 (Winter 1988) pp. 83–103.

Mead, Walter Russell 'American Economic Policy in the Antemillennial Era' in *World Policy Journal*, vol. 6/3 (Summer 1989) pp. 385–468.

Meier, Gerald M. *Problems of a World Monetary Order* 2nd edn (New York: Oxford University Press, 1982).

Minton-Beddoes, Zanny 'Why the IMF Needs Reform' in *Foreign Affairs* (May–June 1995) pp. 123–33.

Moggridge, Donald (ed.) *The Collected Writings of John Maynard Keynes Volume XXVI: Activities 1941–1946, Shaping the Post-War World: Bretton Woods and Reparations* (London: Macmillan and Cambridge, MA: Cambridge University Press, 1980).

Mohammed, Aziz Ali 'A Proposal for Transforming the IMF into a World Central Bank', mimeo (Washington, DC: Washington Center for Policy and Research, 1994).

Montiel, Peter J. and Jonathan D. Ostry 'Targeting the Real Exchange Rate in Developing Countries' in *Finance & Development*, vol. 30/1 (March 1993) pp. 38–40.

Mullineux, A.W. *International Money and Banking: The Creation of a New Order*, especially Chapter 8: 'Do We Need a World Central Bank' (Brighton, UK: Wheatsheaf Books, 1987).

Mundell, Robert A. 'A Theory of Optimum Currency Areas' in *American Economic Review*, vol. 51/4 (September 1961) pp. 657–65.

Mussa, Michael, Morris Goldstein, Peter B. Clark, Donald J.

Mathieson and Tamim Bayoumi *Improving the International Monetary System: Constraints and Possibilities*, IMF Occasional Paper 116 (Washington, DC: IMF, December 1994).

Naim, Moises 'Mexico's Larger Story' in *Foreign Policy*, vol. 112 (Summer 1995) pp. 112–30.

Neu, C. Richard *A New Bretton Woods: Rethinking International Economic Institutions and Arrangements* (Santa Monica, CA: Rand Summer Institute, 1993).

Niehans, Jürg *The Theory of Money* (Baltimore, MA: Johns Hopkins University Press, 1978).

Nurkse, Ragnar 'Conditions of International Monetary Equilibrium' in *Essays in International Finance*, no. 4 (Princeton, NJ: Princeton University Press, 1945).

O'Brien, Richard *Global Financial Integration: The End of Geography* (London: Pinter Publishers, 1992; published in North America for the Royal Institute of International Affairs: New York: Council on Foreign Relations Press, 1992).

Organization for Economic Cooperation and Development (OECD) 'Systemic Risks in Securities Markets' in *Financial Market Trends*, vol. 49 (June 1991) pp. 13–18.

Otani, Yoshito *Ursprung und Lösung des Geldproblems* (Neu Ulm, Germany: Arrow Verlag, 1981).

Preisigke, Friedrich *Girowesen im griechischen Ägypten enthaltend Korngiro, Geldgiro, Girobanknotariat mit Einschluß des Archivwesens* (Strassburg, France: Verlag von Schlesier & Schweikhardt, 1910; reprinted: Hildesheim, Germany and New York: Georg Olms, 1971).

Ricardo, David 'On the Principles of Political Economy, and Taxation' (London: John Murray, 1817) as reprinted in Piero Sraffa (ed.) with the Collaboration of M.H. Dobb *The Works and Correspondence of David Ricardo*, vol. I (Cambridge, England: University Press for the Royal Economic Society, 1951).

Riese, Hajo 'Geldökonomie – Keynes und die Anderen: Kritik der monetären Grundlagen der Orthodoxie' in *Ökonomie und Gesellschaft*, vol. 1: Die Neoklassik und ihre Herausforderungen (Frankfurt, Germany and New York: Campus Verlag, 1983) pp. 103–60.

Rodriguez, Ennio and Stephany Griffith-Jones *Cross-Conditionality, Banking Regulations and Third World Debt: The Experiences of Chile and Mexico* (Basingstoke: Macmillan, 1991).

Rohatyn, Felix and Peter B. Kenen *The Debt Crisis and the World Economy: Report by a Group of Commonwealth Experts* (London: Commonwealth Institute, 1984).

Sachs, Jeffrey D. 'Strengthening IMF Programs in Highly Indebted Countries' in Catherine Gwin and Richard E. Feinberg (eds) *The International Monetary Fund in a Multipolar World: Pulling Together* (New Brunswick, NJ: Transactions Books, 1989) pp. 101–22.

Sachs, Jeffrey D. and Susan M. Collins *Developing Country Debt and Economic Performance* (Chicago, IL: University of Chicago Press, 1989).

Sachs, Jeffrey D. 'A Strategy for Debt Reduction' in *Journal of Economic Perspectives*, vol. 4/1 (Winter 1990) pp. 19–29.

Sachs, Jeffrey and Felipe B. Larrain *Macroeconomics in the Global Economy* (Englewood Cliffs, NJ: Prentice Hall, 1993).

Samuelson, Paul A. 'Nonoptimality of Money Holding under Laissez-Faire' in *Canadian Journal of Economics*, vol. 2/2 (May 1969) pp. 303–8.

Samuelson, Paul A. 'Theoretical Notes on Trade Problems' in *Review of Economics and Statistics*, vol. 46/2 (May 1964) pp. 145–54.

Sen, Sunanda 'Swings and Paradoxes in International Capital Markets: A Theoretical Note' in *Cambridge Journal of Economics*, vol. 15/2 (June 1991) pp. 179–98.

Sen, Sunanda 'Financial Fragility and its World Implications', mimeo (1992).

Sen, Sunanda 'Dimensions of India's External Crisis' in *Economic and Political Weekly*, vol. 29/14 (April 2, 1994) pp. 805–12.

Shelton, Judy *Money Meltdown: Restoring Order to the Global Currency System* (New York: The Free Press, 1994).

Solomon, Robert 'On the Fiftieth Anniversary of Bretton Woods' in *International Economic Letter*, vol. 14 (August 15, 1994) pp. 1–9.

Spahn, Paul Bernd 'International Financial Flows and Transactions Taxes: Survey and Options' in *IMF Working Paper*, WP/95/60 (Washington, DC: IMF, June 1995).

Suhr, Dieter *Geld ohne Mehrwert* (Frankfurt, Germany: Fritz Knapp, 1983).

Suhr, Dieter *Capitalism at Its Best: The Equalisation of Money's Marginal Costs and Benefits* (Augsburg, Germany: Universität Augsburg, 1989).

Suzuki, Yoshio, Junichi Miyake and Mitsuaki Okabe (eds) *The Evolution of the International Monetary System: How Can Efficiency and Stability Be Attained?* (Tokyo: University of Tokyo Press, 1990).

Tarshis, Lorie 'Disarming the International Debt Bomb' in *Challenge*, vol. 30/2 (May–June 1987) pp. 18–23.

Tavlas, George S. 'The Theory of Optimum Currency Areas Revisited' in *Finance & Development*, vol. 30/2 (June 1993) pp. 32–5.

Teunissen, Jan Joost (ed.) *The Pursuit of Reform: Global Finance and Developing Countries* (The Hague: Forum on Debt and Development, FONDAD, 1993).

Tobin, James 'The Interest-Elasticity of Transactions Demand for Cash' in *Review of Economics and Statistics*, vol. 38/3 (August 1956) pp. 241–7.

Tobin, James 'A Proposal for International Monetary Reform' in *Eastern Economic Journal*, vol. 4/3–4 (July–October 1978) pp. 153–9.

Triffin, Robert *Gold and Dollar Crisis* (New Haven, Connecticut: Yale University Press, 1960).

Triffin, Robert 'The Evolution of the International Monetary System: Historical Reappraisal and Future Perspectives' in Princeton Studies in International Finance, no. 12 (Princeton, NJ: Princeton University Press, 1964).

Turvey, Ralph 'Does the Rate of Interest Rule the Roost?' in Frank H. Hahn and F.P.R. Brechling (eds) *Theory of Interest Rates* (London: Macmillan and New York: St Martins, 1965) pp. 164–72.

Ul Hag, Mahbub, Inge Kaul and Isabelle Grunberg (eds) *The Tobin Tax: Coping with Financial Volatility* (New York and Oxford: Oxford University Press, 1996).

United States Department of State *Proceedings and Documents of the United Nations Monetary and Financial Conference, Bretton Woods, NH, July 1–22, 1944* (Washington, DC: United States Government Printing Office, 1948).

United Nations Conference on Trade and Development (UNCTAD) *Trade and Development Report* (New York: United Nations, various years).

United Nations Conference on Trade and Development (UNCTAD) *International Monetary Issues: The International Monetary System and Financial Markets, Recent Developments and the Policy Challenge* (Geneva: UNCTAD, 1984).

United Nations Conference of Trade and Development (UNCTAD) *Compendium of Selected Studies on International Monetary and Financial Issues for the Developing Countries* (New York: United Nations, 1987).

United Nations Conference on Trade and Development (UNCTAD) *International Monetary and Financial Issues for the 1990s: Research Papers for the Group of Twenty-Four*, vols I–VI (New York: United Nations, 1993–95).

United Nations Conference on Trade and Development (UNCTAD) *International Monetary and Financial Issues for the 1990s*, Volume IV, Special Issue, 'Proceedings of a Conference sponsored by the Group of Twenty-Four on the Occasion of the Fiftieth Anniversary of the Bretton Woods Conference' (New York: United Nations, 1994).

United Nations Development Programme (UNDP) *Human Development Report* (New York: Oxford University Press, various years).

Van Dormael, Armand *Bretton Woods: Birth of a Monetary System* (New York: Holmes and Meier Publishers, 1978).

Wachtel, Howard M. *The Money Mandarins: The Making of a Supranational Economic Order*, revised edition (Armonk, NY: M.E. Sharpe and London: Pluto Press, 1990).

Wachtel, Howard M. 'Taming Global Money' in *Challenge*, vol. 38/1 (January–February 1995) pp. 36–40.

Wallace, Neil 'A Legal Restrictions Theory of the Demand for Money and the Role of Monetary Policy' in *Federal Reserve Bank of Minneapolis Quarterly Review*, vol. 7/1 (Winter 1983) pp. 1–7.

White, Lawrence H. 'Accounting for Non-Interest-Bearing Currency: A Critique of the Legal Restrictions Theory of Money' in *Journal of Money, Credit and Banking*, vol. 19/4 (November 1987) pp. 448–56.

Williamson, John 'A Survey of the Literature on the Optimal Peg' in *Journal of Development Economics*, vol. 11/1 (August 1982) pp. 39–61.

Williamson, John *The Exchange Rate System* 2nd edn (Washington, DC: Institute for International Economics, 1985).

Williamson, John 'Exchange Rate Management: The Role of Target Zones' in *American Economic Review*, vol. 77/2 (May 1987) pp. 200–4.

Williamson, John 'Comment on McKinnon's Monetary Rule' in *Journal of Economic Perspectives*, vol. 2/1 (Winter 1988) pp. 113–19.

Williamson, John 'The "Blueprint" Proposals for International Monetary Reform' in Christopher Johnson (ed.) *Changing Exchange Rate Systems* (London: Pinter Publishers, 1990) pp. 30–42.

World Bank, *World Debt Tables* (Washington, DC: World Bank, various years).

World Bank, *World Development Report* (Washington, DC: World Bank, various years).

World Bank *Global Economic Prospects and the Developing Countries* (Washington, DC: World Bank, 1993).

World Institute for Development Economics Research (WIDER) *Foreign Portfolio Investment in Emerging Equity Markets*, Study Group Series no. 5 (Helsinki, Finland: WIDER, 1990).

Yeager, Leland B. 'Essential Properties of the Medium of Exchange', *Kyklos*, vol. 21 (1968) pp. 45–69.

Yeager, Leland B. 'Stable Money and Free Market Currencies', *Cato Journal*, vol. 3/1 (Spring 1983) pp. 305–26.

Notes on Editors and Contributors

Jo Marie Griesgraber is Project Director for the Rethinking Bretton Woods project at the Center of Concern where she has worked on issues related to Third World debt and global economic justice since 1989. She holds a Ph.D. in Political Science from Georgetown University. Her most recent publications include contributions to Lowell S. Gustafson (ed.), *Economic Development Under Democratic Regimes: Neoliberalism in Latin America* (Westport, CT: Praeger, 1994) and 'In the Quest of Systematic Hope: Rethinking Bretton Woods' in *Theology & Public Policy*, vol. 4, no. 2 (Washington, DC: Churches' Center for Theology and Public Policy, Winter 1994) pp. 19–33.

Bernhard G. Gunter has worked with the Rethinking Bretton Woods project as an intern at the Center of Concern. He is a Ph.D. candidate in Economics at the American University, Washington, DC, a member of Pax Christi, Germany, and has focused on global justice since 1980. His most recent publication is 'Financial Crises and the Great Depression in Germany, 1927–1933: A Review with Some New Facts and Arguments' in *Essays in Economic and Business History*, vol. 13 (1995) pp. 55–70.

Robert S. Browne was born in Chicago and holds the BA degree from the University of Illinois and the MBA from the University of Chicago. He has done post-graduate work in economics at the University of Chicago and at the City University of New York. He worked in Indo-China for the US economic aid program from 1955 to 1961, and returned to academia as Assistant Professor of Economics at Fairleigh Dickinson University. From 1969 to 1979, he directed the Black Economic Research Center in New York City, and from 1980 to 1982, he was Executive Director at the African

Development Fund in Abidjan, Cote D'Ivoire, where he represented the United States, the United Kingdom and Yugoslavia. From 1982–85, he was senior research fellow in Howard University's African Studies and Research Program, and from 1986–91, he was the Staff Director of the US House Banking Committee's Subcommittee on International Development, Finance, Trade and Monetary Policy. He was invited by President-elect Clinton to make the presentation on Africa at the Clinton–Gore Economic Summit held in Little Rock, Arkansas, in November 1992. He was a Senior Fellow at Howard University's African Studies Program when writing this chapter and is currently a Senior Research Fellow at the Trans Africa Forum.

Stephany Griffith-Jones holds a Ph.D. from the University of Cambridge. She is a Senior Fellow at the Institute of Development Studies, Sussex University, in the United Kingdom. Previously she worked at the Central Bank of Chile. Recently, she spent eight months working as senior consultant on development finance at the UN Economic Commission for Latin America and the Caribbean (ECLAC). She has acted as senior consultant to many international agencies, including the World Bank, the Inter-American Development ment Bank, the European Economic Community, and the UN Conference on Trade and Development (UNCTAD). She has written widely on international finance, especially in relation to Latin America. Recently, she has written on financial sector reform in transitional economies, as well as on international financial reform and regulation of international private capital flows. Her most recent book (edited with Ricardo Ffrench-Davis) is *Coping with Capital Surges: The Return of Finance to Latin America*, (Boulder, CO: Lynne Rienner, 1995). Her essay 'Institutional Arrangements for a Tax on International currency Transactions' is included in Mahbub Ul Haq, Inge Kaul and Isabelle Grunberg (eds), *The Tobin Tax: Coping with Financial Volatility* (New York and Oxford: Oxford university Press, 1996) pp. 143–58.

Bernard A. Lietaer is a native of Belgium, currently living in California. He is president of Pegasys Currency Fund, an offshore fund based in Cayman that invests exclusively in currencies and gold, and of Pegasys Management Ltd., an investment management firm based in Bermuda. He previously was general manager and currency trader for GaiaCorp, during which time he obtained the highest performance among all offshore currency funds. While heading the organization and planning department of the Belgian Central Bank, he was president of that country's electronic payment system. He also has served as adviser to several Latin American governments and European institutions, as well as major multinational corporations. He received bachelor's and master's degrees in electrical engineering (University of Louvain, Belgium) a master's degree in business administration (MIT), and the position of visiting professor in international finance (University of Louvain).

Bernard Lietaer is author of *Europe + Latin America + the Multinationals: A Positive Sum Game for the Exchange of Raw Materials and Technology* (London: Saxon House, 1979); *Le Grand Jeu Europe Amerique Latine* (Paris: Presses Universitaires de France, 1981) and *Es una oportunidad la deuda?* (Mexico: Fondo de Cultura Economica, 1987).

Avadhoot Nadkarni teaches economics at St Xavier's College, Bombay, and the Department of Economics, University of Bombay. He is also a Fellow at the Social Science Centre of St Xavier's College. His areas of interest include development economics, international economics and econometrics. He has worked on the structural transformation of less-developed countries. His Ph.D. thesis is on 'India's Exchange Rate during the Basket Period (1975–1993)'.

Sunanda Sen is Professor of Economics at the Jawaharlal Nehru University in New Delhi, India. She has been active in developing an alternative point of view on the functioning of the international economy. Her research contests the claims of the 'Washington Consensus,' especially with respect to the impact of international integration on developing nations. Dr Sen has written on the deleterious consequences of 'financial openness' in the industrially advanced economies, reflected in their low output and growth as well as their financial fragility. She also writes on imperialism in the context of colonialism in India.

Her best known work is *Colonies and the Empire: India, 1890–1914* (Calcutta: Orient Longmans, 1992). She has published papers on international finance and related disciplines in a number of edited volumes and international journals. Her forthcoming books include *Fragile Finance: Debt and Economic Reform,* (ed.) (Macmillan) and *India: Controls, Liberalization and Deregulation in the External Sector* (Sage Publications).

Rethinking Bretton Woods

PROJECT SPONSORS
* Personal Capacity, organization listed for identification only.

Charles Abugre
Third World Network
GHANA

Adebayo Adedeji
African Centre for Development and Strategic Studies
NIGERIA

Peggy Antrobus
Development Alternatives with Women for a New Era (DAWN)
BARBADOS

Tissa Balasuriya, OMI
Centre for Society and Religion
SRI LANKA

David Barkin *
Lincoln Institute of Land Policy
Cambridge, MA and MEXICO

Leonor Briones
Freedom from Debt Coalition
PHILIPPINES

Edward Broadbent and **David Gillies**
International Centre for Human Rights
and Democratic Development
CANADA

Salvie D. Colina
Asian Center for the Progress of Peoples
HONG KONG

Sarath Fernando
Devasarana Development Centre
SRI LANKA

Susan Fleck and **Bernhard Gunter**
Economics Graduate Student Union
The American University
Washington, DC USA

Louis Goodman
Dean, School of International Service
The American University
Washington, DC USA

J. Bryan Hehir *
Harvard University
Cambridge, MA USA

Gabriel Izquierdo, SJ
Centro de Investigacion y Educacion Popular (CINEP)
COLOMBIA

Fatima Mello
Federation of Organizations for Social and
Educational Assistance (FASE)
BRAZIL

Guy Mhone
Southern Africa Regional Institute for Policy Studies
ZIMBABWE

Luis Peirano and **Humberto Campodonico**
Centro de Estudios y Promocion
del Desarrollo (DESCO)
PERU

Sebasti L. Raj, SJ
Indian Social Institute
INDIA

Jorge Sabato *
Centro de Estudios Avanzados
ARGENTINA

Francisco Sagasti
Grupo de Analisis para el Desarrollo (GRADE)
PERU

Tom Schlesinger
Southern Finance Project
Philomont, VA USA

Kavaljit Singh
Public Interest Research Group
INDIA

Rob van Drimmelen
World Council of Churches
SWITZERLAND

Peter van Tuijl and **Augustinus Rumansara**
International NGO Forum on Indonesian Development
INDONESIA / THE NETHERLANDS

Layashi Yaker
United Nations Economic Commission for Africa
ETHIOPIA

Noel Keizo Yamada, SJ
Sophia University
JAPAN

PROJECT ADVISORY GROUP

Nii Akwuettah
Africa Development Foundation

Nancy Alexander
Bread for the World Institute

Steven Arnold
Professor, School of International Service
The American University

Ambassador **Richard Bernal**
Embassy of Jamaica

Daniel Bradlow
Professor, Washington College of Law
The American University

Robert Browne
Economic Consultant

Margaret Crahan
Luce Professor of Religion, Power and Political Process
Occidental College, Los Angeles

Maria Floro
Professor, Department of Economics
The American University

Louis Goodman
Dean, School of International Service
The American University

Jo Marie Griesgraber
Project Director, Center of Concern

Chandra Hardy
International Development Training Institution

James E. Hug, SJ
Director, Center of Concern

Constantine Michalopoulos
The World Bank

Moises Naim
Senior Fellow, Carnegie Endowment for International Peace

Ambassador **Margaret Taylor**
Embassy of Papua New Guinea

Marijke Torfs
Friends of the Earth/USA

Index

Index by Auriol Grifith-Jones